THE
PAST DISPLAYED

A Journey Through the Ancient World

THE PAST DISPLAYED

Courtlandt Canby

PHAIDON · OXFORD

Phaidon Press Limited
Littlegate House, St Ebbe's Street, Oxford

First published 1980
Planned and produced by
Elsevier Publishing Projects (UK) Limited, Oxford

Copyright © 1980
Elsevier International Projects, Amsterdam

ISBN 0 7148 1915 8

Editors: Bernard Dod, Bill MacKeith
Design: Gwyn Lewis
Picture editor: Christine Forth
Production: Ivor Parker
Index: Elizabeth Scott Glover

Filmset by
Keyspools Limited, Golborne, Lancashire

Printed by
Officine Grafiche di
Arnoldo Mondadori Editore, Verona

CONTENTS

CHRONOLOGY

References in **bold** indicate topics dealt with in this volume.

	THE NEAR EAST	EGYPT AND NORTH AFRICA	THE GREEK WORLD	ITALY AND ROME	ELSEWHERE IN EUROPE	INDIA AND PAKISTAN
					Palaeolithic figure carvings and cave paintings c 30,000–11,000 BC / c 11,000 end of Ice Age	
10,000 BC	earliest settled villages, herding, pottery, crop cultivation; towns at Jericho, Catal Huyuk copper used before 6000 **Hassuna ware (6000),**	agricultural settlements, farming, pottery, domestication of animals widespread in SE, Mediterranean, W				
5000 BC	**Samarra, Halaf, Ubaid and Uruk (to 3000) ware in Mesopotamia** / Sumer cities develop; bronze casting; writing	c 3100 unification of			from c 4500 great stone monuments and tombs in W, especially Brittany; copper artefacts in Balkans	
3000 BC		Upper and Lower Egypt / Old Kingdom 3rd and 4th dynasties (c 2686–2494) **great pyramids built**	early Bronze Age Cycladic culture in Aegean		**Ireland: Boyne valley graves (to c 2000)** spread of metal technology with Beaker culture (to c 2000)	growth of Indus valley civilization (to 1500)
2500 BC	c 2500 **Royal cemetery of Ur**					
2000 BC	Assyrian and Babylonian states founded. / Hittite empire in Anatolia (to 1200 BC)	Middle Kingdom (20C–18C) / New Kingdom 18th dynasty	**palace civilizations of Crete c 1930–1400: Knossos etc.** shaft graves of Mycenae **Minoan civilization on Thera: frescoes**	Appenine culture	**great sarsen stones erected at Stonehenge** most megalithic monuments raised c 2000–1500	
1500 BC	Hittite empire break-up / iron technology spreads	(c 1567–1320): **building of the great temples. Tutankhamun c 1347–1338** / Phoenicians spread west	c 1400 Knossos destroyed			Aryans invade India
1000 BC	beginning of Jewish religion. / Assyrian empire at its most powerful / c 550 Cyrus founds Persian	through Mediterranean; Carthage founded 814 / c 525 Persians conquer	colonies established in east and (from 8C) west **the oracle of Apollo at Delphi at the height of its influence (7C–6C)**	Villanovan culture in N 753 Rome founded c 750 first Greek colonies **Etruscan civilization at**	Early Iron ("Hallstatt") Age (to 500 BC) / Late Iron Age ("La Tène"	Aryans expand E and S Vedic texts (900–400) / Magadha and Kosala
500 BC	empire; **Persepolis built c 520–420** Seleucus I (d 280) of Syria / Parthian empire (247 BC–224 AD)	Egypt / Ptolemy I of Egypt (304–284) / Egypt becomes province	Greeks repulse Persians **Athens: age of Pericles** Alexander (356–323) conquers as far as India **Delos a political and trading center (5C–1C)**	its peak; tombs of Cerveteri Roman republic (founded c 500) dominates Italy, then Mediterranean Augustus first emperor	period); **Butser Hill Farm simulates period**	kingdoms (6C–4C) 489 death of Buddha Chandragupta founds Mauryan dynasty, expels Greeks (321–300) **Ajanta cave sanctuaries**
0	c 30 AD death of Christ / Sasanian empire (c. 224–640); **rock carvings of kings (to 510; also 7C)**	of Rome	86 BC Romans sack Athens	(27 BC–14 AD) **79 AD Pompeii buried** 117 empire at greatest extent 410 Vizigoths sack Rome 476 end of Western Roman	5C–6C Germanic, Slav invasions; 486 Clovis	**(c 200 BC–c 650 AD) 1C–3C Kushan dynasty in Gandhara (NW Pakistan): sculptures and reliefs. 4C–6C Hindu art flowers**
500 AD	632 death of Muhammad Arab expansion begins 750 Abbasid caliphate replaces Umayyads.	Arabs take over North Africa (8C–11C)	718 Arabs beseige Constantinople	empire	founds Frank kingdom / 711 Arabs in France 800 Charlemagne emperor 10C–13C Kievian state	**under Gupta dynasty in N, Pallava dynasty (to 8C) in S; great temples built in 7C** 8C–1296 Pala dynasty in NE
1000 AD	1055 Seljuks in Baghdad 1096 First Crusade / 1258 Mongols sack Baghdad	1250–1517 Mamlūks rule Egypt **1356 Mosque of Sultan**	1071 Seljuks defeat Byzantium / 1453 Ottoman Turks take		Normans conquer England (1066) and S Italy / 13C Mongols invade E / Ivan III (1440–1505)	Muslims invade / 13C–14C Delhi sultanate
1500 AD	1516–17 Ottomans overrun Syria, Egypt, Arabia	**Hasan, Cairo, begun**	Constaninople		founds Russian state	1526–1857 Moghul empire

SOUTHEAST ASIA, BURMA, THAILAND	CHINA	JAPAN	THE AMERICAS	AFRICA EXCLUDING THE NORTH	
			radiocarbon dates for sites of hunting people 25,000–17,000 BC in Canada, Mexico, Andes	pebble-tools found date back 2.4m years	
		c 10,000 simple pottery. Jōmon period	7000–5000 beginnings of domestication of plants in Mesoamerica		10,000 BC
rice cultivation in		coastal fishing, seafood collecting			
Thailand					5000 BC
	c 4000 earliest farming settlements in N and NW				
bronze used in Thailand		clustered pit dwellings, elaborate pottery			
			first known pottery in N of South America, Mesoamerica; copper artefacts at Great Lakes	arable farming spreads south	3000 BC
					2500 BC
				Sahara begins to become desert	
		stone circles in N	pottery in SE of North America		2000 BC
	Shang dynasty (Bronze Age culture) c 1500–1027				1500 BC
			1150–900 climax of Olmec		1000 BC
	Chou dynasty 1027–227	population declining	culture in Mexico		
	iron technology enters 520 death of Lao-tsu			**Nok culture, N Nigeria (to 3C AD): terracottas** c 600 Meroë capital of	
	479 death of Confucius glazed pottery 221–206 Shi Huang Ti unites China, builds first Great Wall **206 BC–220 AD Han dynasty: tombs of Liu Sheng and Tou**	c 300 Yao period begins rice, barley cultivated bronze, then iron, introduced	first pyramids in Mexico	Cush kingdom (11C BC–4C AD) iron technology spreads to Niger region beginnings of Ethiopia state	500 BC
spread of Buddhist centers and Indian influence 2C–17C Cham kingdom (modern Vietnam) 3C–6C Funan kingdom, Mekong delta region	**Wan, Lady T'ai** Buddhism, Taoism spread c 300 Huns invade 316–581 North and South dynasties: classic age in poetry and painting	from Korea first large tumuli 5C Yamato state established	300–900 classic Maya period	Aksum empire (to 8C) in N Ethiopia early Iron Age culture in Mozambique, Zimbabwe,	0
Mon kingdoms in S Burma and Thailand 616 Khmer kingdom founded (to 15C) c 800 temples of Borobudur, Java, built	618–906 T'ang dynasty, 2nd classic age in arts, incl. **tomb figurines, painting** 960–1279 Sung dynasty:	6C Chinese influence increases Buddhism in Japan 710 Nara period begins 794 Kyoto replaces Nara as capital	Pueblo cliff dwellers	Zambia with the Bantus 6C kingdom of Ghana founded Arab cities on E coast **Ife flourishes 900–1400**	500 AD
11C–13C Burmese kingdom of Pagan **Angkor Wat built** early Sukothai (13C–14C) and Ayuthia (14C–18C) dynasties in Thailand	**masters of landscape** 13C Mongols invade 1275 M. Polo in China 1368–1644 Ming dynasty; **tomb figurines; 1405–20 Forbidden City built**	9C–12C Fujiwara dominate the court 1192–3 Yoritomo, military dictator, ends imperial rule	c 1100 bronze casting in Bolivia c 1200 beginning of Chimu civilization, Peru Inca and Aztec empires at their height	1200 gold mined in SE Mali, Songhai, empires **14C–15C Great Zimbabwe built** 1400–1800 Benin city	1000 AD
	1644 Manchu dynasty (to 1912)		**15C Machu Picchu built**	Songhai empire at peak Portuguese, then Dutch, English, French settle	1500 AD
		19C Meiji resoration; Shinto becomes state cult			

INTRODUCTION

Formal history is usually said to begin with the earliest written records and, for reasons of convenience, may be said to end perhaps in the 1950s (though museums may anticipate formal history, as did the Smithsonian Institution by the prompt exhibition of the space capsules of the 1960s). The past, however, as displayed in this book, begins with the emergence of *Homo sapiens* and floods forward to the present. It is part of the limitless sea upon which we make our voyage, rolling aeons behind us and out of sight ahead.

But while the future can only be guessed at, the past (to change the metaphor) can be quarried to find out how we climbed to our present perilous eminence, and why. Nuggets of it can be dug out, as in this book, raised to the full light of the present and examined for what they will reveal. The answers will never be very exact but may help at least to widen the mind's horizons, and may even serve as a yardstick with which to measure the events of the present. Then, too, lovers of the past must admit that adventuring among the oddities and surprises of the past is also diverting. To delve among the hundreds of photographs spanning continents and millennia in this volume should prove stimulating and exciting, each of the 30 chapters providing a brief package tour to foreign parts without the attendant headaches and discomforts of travel.

But in mining the past, where is one to dig? Wherever one probes there is something of interest – the sudden and total collapse of the brilliant young civilizations of the Aegean, contrasted with the stubborn, almost dogged persistence of those of China or Egypt over thousands of years; the enticements of traditional dance in Indian Asia; the unexpected arrogance of the Athenians who founded Western civilization. This book is not a systematic survey of world history. What it does attempt to convey is the variety and range of ancient cultures by taking the reader, for example, on an eye-catching tour around one of the world's great archaeological sites, or by focussing on a high point in the achievements of a culture, such as the pyramids – monuments to the early pharoahs of Egypt – or the sculptures of West Africa. Some of the topics of the thirty picture-essays have been chosen because they seem to have some particular relevance to the present, others because they illuminate some little-known facet of the past or throw new light on an already familiar story. The attentive reader will note the many interesting cross-relations between one topic and another – the intense awareness of most early people, whether in Ireland, Peru or elsewhere, of the importance of nature and of the sun, moon and stars which can bring them either disaster or well-being, or the uncanny parallels between the long-lived civilizations of China and of Egypt.

Each of the six parts of the book presents a major aspect of past civilization, either in a culture's own terms or in relation to the present. Within these, each chapter has an introduction which relates its subject to the history and archaeology of the period, before exploring the subject in greater detail through photographs, drawings, diagrams, maps and reconstructions. First we look at six great cities which have been rediscovered and investigated in modern times. Part Two visits five great religious centers and discusses the nature of their importance in bygone days. In Part Three we tour the monuments and palaces of great dynasties, and in Part Four the commemoration of the dead as a central feature of civilization is examined. Some outstanding landmarks in the history of painting and sculpture are illustrated in Part Five and, with Part Six, we turn to the present. Some of our past, even though brought to light by archaeologists and art historians, may be dead and buried; but in the continuing practice of ancient Shinto rites in Japan, in formal Hindu dance, and in the work of Turkish and Afghan potters whose methods go back to prehistory, we have concrete examples of the continuity between past and present. The final chapter documents an exciting experiment in attempting to recreate in our day the life on an Iron Age farm over 2,000 years ago.

The reader will find much emphasis throughout on archaeology, because during the last century this fascinating discipline, while filling in many details of known history, has also been responsible for the uncovering of an entirely new past, a past that extends backward in time beyond the written records to disclose the complex growth of human culture from the beginning. Like their fellow scientists, the archaeologists have been working along the frontiers of knowledge, throwing new light on what it has meant to be human. Problems, as in any new discipline, have arisen, some of which are touched on in this book – the revolution in radiocarbon dating methods, which has placed the megalithic monuments of Western Europe (like Stonehenge) earlier rather than later than their supposed prototypes in the Aegean, or a new awareness of the distortions brought about by the excavation of material remains alone – since the tombs, palaces and monuments of the past were usually the work of the elite. To pin down something about the life of the ordinary citizen there is a new emphasis on settlement patterns, population studies and a more careful interpretation of the lesser remains. In fact, thanks primarily to archaeology and anthropology, historical studies now tend to emphasize the growth of culture and the origins of civilization rather than the kings, battles and politics of the past. You will find much of the former in this book.

Here, then, is a sampling of the riches of the past, displayed for your entertainment and edification. May the book please those who are already familiar with the past, and perhaps lead others to a further exploration of the treasures they may find there for themselves.

Courtlandt Canby

PART ONE

Lost Cities

POMPEII

A Roman city buried by Vesuvius

Vesuvius broods over Pompeii and the bay of Naples, as Dickens wrote, "like the doom and destiny of this beautiful country, biding its time." It has erupted many times, the last in 1944, but the most famous occasion of all was on August 24, 79 AD, when it overwhelmed Pompeii, Herculaneum and other Roman towns at its base. Pompeii, a busy mercantile city somewhat inland, was buried deep in ashes and pumice; Herculaneum, an aristocratic seaside retreat, was covered by molten lava and mud. Premonitory earthquakes in 62 and 63, which heavily damaged both cities, were ignored. Herculaneum was the worst damaged, but both cities were extensively rebuilt. The only warning of the catastrophe of 79 was, as Dio Cassius wrote, fearful bellowing noises from beneath the ground. Then there was a shattering crash, huge rocks were hurled aloft, and a mushroom cloud began to form above the mountain, hiding the sun.

Even in Misenum, more than 10 miles away across the bay, the midday sky was black with ash-laden smoke. We have a vivid account of the eruption by the 17-year-old Pliny the Younger, who was at Misenum with his mother at the time. Resolving to leave the town, they were "followed by a panic-stricken mob of people ... who hurried us on our way by pressing hard behind in a dense crowd ... The carriages we had ordered to be brought out began to run in different directions, though the ground was quite level, and would not remain stationary even when wedged with stones. We also saw the sea sucked away and apparently forced back by the earthquake ... On the landward side a fearful black cloud was rent by forked and quivering bursts of flame, and parted to reveal great tongues of fire, like flashes of lightning magnified in size ... Soon afterwards the cloud sank down to earth and covered the sea; it had already blotted out Capri and hidden the promontory of Misenum ... Ashes were

already falling, not as yet very thickly. I looked around: a dense black cloud was coming up behind us, spreading over the earth ... We had scarcely sat down to rest when darkness fell, not the dark of a moonless or cloudy night, but as if the lamp had been put out in a closed room. You could hear the shrieks of women, the wailing of infants, and the shouting of men; some were calling their parents, others their children or their wives, trying to recognize them by their voices."

Pliny and his mother survived, but in Pompeii, taken unawares, there were tragic scenes, as we know from the skilled excavations. The skeletons of a family were found lying together, two adults holding hands and at their feet two children clasped arm-in-arm in death. Of the gladiators, 63 had died in their barracks, some chained together at the ankles. In the temple of Isis, hastily deserted by its priests, the bones of an animal, just sacrificed when the eruption came, lay on the altar and in another room a carbonized meal was found – eggs, fruit and nuts that were never eaten. Even the shapes of the victims have been recovered by filling the cavities left by their bodies with plaster – a dog twisting against its chain, a man sprawled face down, his fists clenched in agony. Many, however, must have escaped, on foot or on animals, for few ridable animals were found in the city.

After the catastrophe Pompeii lay buried under a hill of pumice later called Città; Herculaneum had vanished altogether. Soon both cities were forgotten. The thick layer of volcanic material discouraged casual exploration. For 1600 years there was silence, until the probing of wells and canals in the 17th century brought up rich marbles, inscriptions and mosaics. Even then the finds were not always recognized for what they were. Crude excavations, using galley slaves, and gunpowder where possible, commenced in the 18th century. Herculaneum was discovered first, and the finds were brought to the notice of the world in a series of lavish volumes produced by the court at Naples. After much uncertainty, Pompeii was finally recognized as the long-lost city, and more treasures began to appear. So sumptuous were the objects

Opposite Detail from the fine frescoes in the Villa of Mysteries, built on the outskirts of Pompeii about 60 BC. It is thought that these paintings may show the initiation of a bride or brides in the Dionysiac mysteries.

uncovered that all Europe, amazed, began to realize that
here was a discovery unlike any other, and soon the great
and gifted from all the world – Horace Walpole, Boswell,
Goethe, Humboldt, Melville, Scott – began to flock to the
sites to be taken by torchlight through the tunnels dug
into Herculaneum or to view Pompeii in the open air. The
buried cities began to find their way into the arts and
literature of Europe.

It was not until 1860, when G. Fiorelli became director,
that the excavations were put on a systematic basis. Today
excavation continues in Pompeii, Herculaneum and the
villas around them; but with refined techniques the houses
are being restored *in situ*, much as they were in the 1st
century, so that little is left to the imagination. What does
this recreated Pompeii tell us about itself? The remains
reveal every detail of a bustling commercial city of
generally small and crowded houses – a lusty, bawdy city
(or a crudely dissolute one according to one's point of
view) – for the sexuality of some of the statues, paintings
and objects is open and blatant. Pompeii was a provincial
city of the early Empire, reflecting much of the
sophisticated life of Rome under Nero and his immediate
successors, but also the refined tastes of Greek-influenced
southern Italy. It had been an Etruscan and a Samnite city
and with Herculaneum had rebelled against Rome as late
as the 80s BC, and was besieged by the bloody dictator,
Sulla, in 89 BC.

The sheer variety and abundance of the finds at Pompeii
is breathtaking, ranging from the spaciousness of the
House of the Faun (or the enormous villa recently
excavated at Oplontis which may have belonged to
Poppaea, Nero's wife), to the homely details of corner
food shops, bakeries, brothels and latrines. The walls are
scratched with lovers' messages, obscenities, election
propaganda: The Muleteers support C. Julius Polybius
for Praetor! Many have loved Pompeii, many more have
been repelled by it. "This mummified city," Goethe called
it, while the aging Sir Walter Scott was heard to mutter
"City of the Dead, City of the Dead" as he walked its
streets. Shelley, after his visit to the ruins, caught a
properly elegiac mood:

> I stood within the city disinterred:
>   And heard the autumnal leaves
>   like light footfalls
> Of spirits passing through the
>   streets; and heard
>   The Mountain's slumberous voice
>   at intervals
>   Thrill the roofless halls . . .

Right The view southeast from the Tower of Mercury, on the
northern city wall, towards the center of Pompeii, including the
Forum, which lies beyond the arches at the end of the street in the
picture.

Above Vesuvius, deceptively peaceful, rises over Pompeii and the entrance to the Forum. The Temple of Jupiter is on the left. The Forum, with its temples and Basilica (a large hall for public business), was the religious and commercial center of the city.

Right An ordinary street in Pompeii, showing the unpretentious exterior of the houses. With their pillared gardens and frescoed walls, they could be quite grandiose inside. The house on the left has been reconstructed from the remains preserved under the thick layer of volcanic ash.

Opposite The small covered theater at Pompeii, built between 80 and 75 BC, held no more than 1,500 spectators. It was used for musical recitals and mimes. During the earthquake of 62 AD, the emperor Nero was performing an opera in such a theater at nearby Naples, and ordered the audience to remain in their seats till he had finished.

Above The interior of a Pompeian house. The central court or *atrium* was open to the sky, and in the center there was usually a pool with perhaps a fountain. The floor was covered with mosaics. Leading away from the *atrium* can be seen the open dining room overlooking the garden. The grander Roman villas often had a colonnaded portico surrounding a formal garden (see opposite).

Right The ruins of the Basilica, which stood in the Forum, close to the city's main temples. The equivalent of a bank and a stock exchange today, it was the bustling center of commercial Pompeii with its many markets and shops. One wealthy man, Julius Felix, was the owner of 90 shops, all of which he rented out.

The architecture and decoration of Pompeii and Herculaneum have inspired many later imitations. The J. Paul Getty Museum at Malibu, California (**top**), is based on the Villa of the Papyri at Herculaneum, while the walls of the inner peristyle reproduce First Style decoration from the House of the Faun at Pompeii. The designs for the early 19th-century wall paintings in the Residenz at Munich (**left**) are derived from Third Style decorations at Pompeii and the 18th-century fan (**above**), a tourist souvenir, is based on a fresco at Herculaneum. (See overleaf for a commentary on styles.)

The frescoes of Pompeii are among the best-preserved Roman wall decorations that have survived. They are not masterpieces, but in general reflect middlebrow taste in a Roman country town, echoing the fashions of Rome without being original themselves. Their discovery in the 18th century gave a powerful stimulus to the developing Neoclassical movement, and they have exerted considerable influence on European and American interior decoration (see previous page).

In 1882 August Mau divided Pompeian frescoes into four styles, categories which are now applied to all Roman wall decorations of the period c. 200 BC–79 AD. The First Style merely imitated in colored plaster the marble slabs which decorated the walls of rich Hellenistic Greek houses. This style was reproduced on the inner walls of the courtyard in the J. Paul Getty Museum, illustrated on a previous page, deriving from the Pompeian House of the Faun.

The Second Style, probably based on stage scenery, reached Pompeii when it became a Roman colony in 80 BC, and can be seen on the walls of the Villa of Mysteries (**right**). By the imposition of columns and projecting architraves an impression of depth is created. The fresco illustrated on p. 14 dates from the Second Style period. The Third Style came to Rome by 12 BC, and is first found on the walls of the villa at Boscoreale (**below right**), built in 11 BC for Agrippa Postumus. The architectural elements have become slender and dainty; the bases and capitals of the columns have almost disappeared and the decorative elements are becoming fanciful. In the Fourth Style, which appeared in Pompeii after the earthquake of 62 AD, the trend towards fantasy and the theatrical is intensified, reflecting the decadence of Nero's Rome; it can be seen in the frescoes in the Garden Room of the House of the Vettii (**opposite**). Though architectural elements reappear, the columns have now become spindly twirls and slender scrolls. The wall paintings were intended to give an illusion of space in the rather small houses of Pompeii.

Opposite above Bread was the principal element in the Pompeian diet and there were several bakeries in the city. In one an oven was found which still contained about 80 loaves. The bakeries were frequently equipped with a mill room such as the one illustrated here. The grain was poured in at the top and was crushed as a donkey turned the upper stone, harnessed to a shaft through the holes. The flour issued out below.

Far left As the people fled from the catastrophe they left behind their unfinished meals. These dishes of carbonized eggs, hazelnuts, almonds and dates and a loaf of bread are now in the Pompeii museum.

Left There were many snack bars (*thermopolia*) in Pompeii, as well as wine bars, all open to the street. In this bar the food was kept warm in containers set into the counter. The noisy, crowded streets of Pompeii 1,900 years ago must have been very much like those of nearby Naples today. Pompeian graffiti

scrawled all over the walls – election slogans, dirty jokes – help bring the ruins back to life.

Above left A terracotta statue of Jupiter, found with a statue of Juno and a bust of Minerva (the Roman triad of gods) in the inner sanctuary of the Temple of Zeus Meilichios which served as their temple after the earthquake of 62 AD. In the Greek and Roman world gods often shared temples, usually with one as the leading deity. Though the Romans had their own gods, many of them were equated with the Greek gods who lived on Mount Olympus. Thus Jupiter was considered the same as the Greek Zeus, father of the gods. The above statue of Jupiter is probably a copy of a Greek statue of Zeus, but the fact that it is of terracotta rather than marble or bronze is reminiscent of the Etruscans, from whom the Romans inherited much of their culture: the Etruscans' statues of their gods were commonly fashioned in terracotta (fired clay). Cults from other lands were also popular in the Greco-Roman world

and Pompeii had its temple of Isis, the Egyptian goddess, whose priests were overcome by the eruption as they fled with the altar furnishings of their temple, leaving the uneaten meal of fruit, eggs and nuts behind them.

Above right The courtyard of the Temple of Apollo was surrounded by a Doric portico. A replica of a statue of the god stands in front of it. Statuary was popular in Roman cities, and many fine examples, especially those found in Herculaneum, were copies of Greek works.

GREAT ZIMBABWE

African royal capital

When in the years 1497–98 the Portuguese explorer, Vasco da Gama, rounded the Cape of Good Hope and sailed up Africa's east coast, he was astonished at what he found. There were thriving cities, as populous and as civilized as those he had left behind in Portugal. Kilwa, he reported, had "many fair houses of stones and mortar with many windows after our fashion, very well arranged in streets." The inhabitants, black Swahilis with a few Arabs, were sophisticated and wary. The harbors were crowded with shipping, the sailors' charts and navigational aids were as good as – if not better than – his own, and the natives made it clear that they were familiar with ships much larger than his puny caravels. The wealth of these cities, the Portuguese found, arose from a lucrative trade in gold and ivory from the interior, exchanged for "colored cloths and beads." The gold and ivory were exported to Arabia, the Persian Gulf, India and even far-off China. Determined to control this trade for themselves, the Portuguese soon returned to pillage and raid the coastal cities, which they eventually subdued. But not until the 17th century were they able to explore the interior and eventually control parts of it, for it was hostile and the terrain was difficult. Nor could the coastal people, when the Portuguese first arrived, tell them much about the interior. Fifteen or 20 days' journey inland, they told the Portuguese in 1517, "lies the great kingdom of Benametapa" (Monomotapa) whose king lives in "a very large building" in "a great town called Zimboache." Thus the stone ruins of Great Zimbabwe, in southeast Zimbabwe (formerly Rhodesia), entered history – European history, that is.

For until recent years Africa south of the Sahara was not supposed to have had any history before the arrival of the Europeans. This attitude was a heritage from the 19th-century European colonialists, who found the Africans indolent and backward and their culture stagnant – not realizing how much this was due to their colonial predecessors, starting with the Portuguese. As late as 1961 an eminent British historian wrote, "At present there is no

African history, there is only the history of the Europeans in Africa, the rest is darkness ...". Africa showed no "purposive movement"; why therefore, he wondered, should people amuse themselves with "the unrewarding gyrations of barbarous tribes in picturesque but irrelevant corners of the globe"? Since the 1950s, however, African history has been rescued, and has been studied in its own terms. For instance, the reasons for Africa's "backwardness" in comparison with Europe and Asia are now understood: isolation, a hostile environment, and the interference of Europeans just when Africa was beginning to develop. Distances in Africa are vast, communications poor, few rivers are navigable and much of the land is desert or forest, hostile to settlement. There were few permanent settlements south of the Sahara until near the beginning of the Christian era, and states and kingdoms only began to develop in Africa within the last thousand years or so. Then came the slave traders and the European colonists to disrupt their progress.

Because African history has so recently become a subject of study by Europeans, and is so utterly different from other histories, many people have refused to admit that there is such a thing, and have confidently asserted, for instance, that a massive ruin like Great Zimbabwe could never have been built by blacks and must therefore be the work of the Phoenicians, of the Egyptians – or perhaps it was the Queen of Sheba's palace. The careful work of the new historians, however, aided by archaeology, has begun to establish the truth. History in the east and south of Africa began with the slow spread of the Bantu-speaking peoples in the early centuries AD from their homeland in eastern Nigeria into an almost empty subcontinent. They brought with them the use of iron, and by the time that the first permanent settlement was established at Great Zimbabwe in the 11th century AD, the Bantu-speaking Shona peoples of the neighboring area had established a stable society based on agriculture, the raising of cattle and the use of iron implements. Goldmining, a seasonal occupation, was the basis of foreign trade; the gold was exchanged with Swahili traders from the coastal cities of Sofala and Kilwa at great

Opposite An aerial view of Great Zimbabwe, looking south. In the background is the Elliptical Building.

inland fairs, one of which was undoubtedly held at or near Great Zimbabwe; and the wealth so obtained was not used for productive purposes but rather for the glorification of the "divine chief" and his entourage. Thus the great buildings at Zimbabwe (which means chief's house) were built for the most part during the late 14th and early 15th centuries to celebrate the king's power and glory at the height of his prosperity, when this great palace or tribal center was the capital of a vast kingdom. Its maze of stone walls, now a meaningless jumble, never bore roofs but was built to back up and shelter circular clay-walled huts in the manner of all traditional African compounds; and here lived, worked and worshiped the king and his relatives, governors, priests and bureaucrats. So Zimbabwe after all was a purely African creation, although its wealth depended indirectly upon the Indian Ocean trade. For instance, a bizarre hoard dug up in 1902 included royal insignia, ornate jewelry, iron hoes, innumerable trade goods and beads, objects of gold, iron, copper and bronze as well as Syrian glass, a Persian bowl and Chinese vessels.

By the time the Portuguese arrived Great Zimbabwe had already lost its economic dominance; the kingdom had fragmented into a number of rival states, including the Monomotapa in the north, who became trading partners of the Portuguese in the 16th century. But the Great Zimbabwe culture survived, for Great Zimbabwe was only the largest among at least 80 other lesser zimbabwes, or stone enclosures, which have been found on the great granite plateau, dating from the same period. Great Zimbabwe remained in use as a settlement, though its supremacy had gone. In 1693 one of the southern Shona states actually swept the Portuguese and their Monomotapa allies from the plateau, and Shona rule survived there until the 1830s, when Great Zimbabwe and the other Shona palaces were reduced to lonely ruins by the savage onslaught of Nguni nomadic bands, who had pushed north to escape the militant Zulus and the encroaching Dutch Boers. The Nguni caught the last Shona king and flayed him alive.

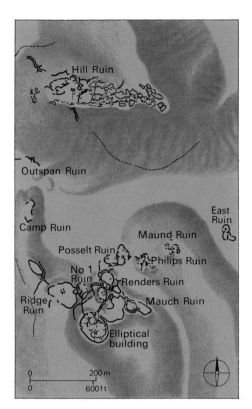

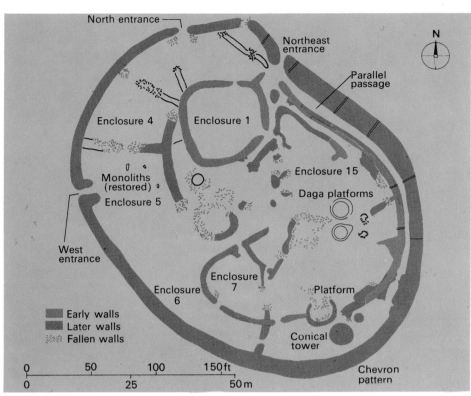

Above A sketch map of the Great Zimbabwe site, showing the principal remains. Zimbabwe was never a fortress; it grew haphazardly as a trading center and focus of royal power.

Left Zimbabwe in its setting of wooded hills with outcrops of rocks. This view of the dominating Elliptical Building is taken from the Hill Ruin, built on an outcrop that overlooks the site.

Below The enigmatic Conical Tower is the most imposing structure in the Elliptical Building. It was interpreted by Victorian antiquarians as a phallic symbol, but in fact its shape is reminiscent of the traditional Shona farmer's granary.

Above Plan of the Elliptical Building. The earliest part of the building was Enclosure 1, probably built early in the 14th century, with an encircling wall outside it. This was supplemented at the height of Zimbabwe's prosperity in the 15th century by a massive outer wall, part of which runs parallel to the old wall. The purpose of the platforms of *daga* (clay) and stone monoliths is not known.

Below The eastern section of the outer wall, having been the latest built, is the most imposing, 35 feet high and 17 feet thick. Note the chevron pattern in the upper courses and the monolithic stones capping the wall. No mortar was used in any of the walls of Great Zimbabwe.

Top left   The oldest walls of the Hill Ruin are built on and around the natural boulders of the site. The earliest dwellings were found on the Hill.

Above left   The wall of the Western Enclosure of the Hill Ruin, showing the masonry "turrets" and one of the granite monoliths set in the top of the wall. These presumably had some ritual function.

Top right   The Hill Ruin, looking westwards. In the Eastern Enclosure in the foreground carved soapstone columns, dishes and small human figurines were found. It was perhaps a religious area. In the Western Enclosure in the background the accumulated settlement deposits were 15 feet thick, the oldest dating from the 11th and 12th centuries.

Above right   A detail of the wall of the Elliptical Building reveals a sophisticated and aesthetically pleasing method of creating steps out of successive courses of masonry.

Right   Some of the granite monoliths built into the wide top of the outer wall of the Elliptical Building.

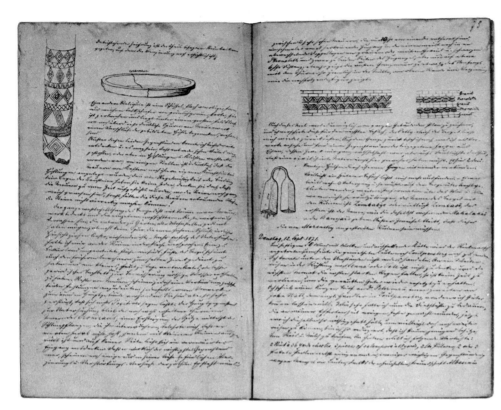

Above A page from the diary of the German explorer and geologist Karl Mauch (depicted **right**), describing his visit to Great Zimbabwe on September 11, 1871. Mauch lived in the area for nearly nine months, mapping the ruins and finding objects of metal and carved stone. The objects drawn in the diary include a carved stone column, a soapstone dish, a gong and details of the chevron pattern in the masonry of the walls. The two objects **below** are a gong of the type seen by Mauch and a soapstone dish found at Great Zimbabwe, depicting baboons, a man with a dog on a leash, and zebras. The gong puzzled Mauch, and he wrote: "Its use was a complete riddle to me, but it proves that a civilized nation once must have lived here." Mauch believed that the ruins at Great Zimbabwe were a copy of the original palace of the Queen of Sheba. The imperialist Cecil Rhodes, who preferred to think of Zimbabwe as Phoenician, bought Mauch's relics and later sent an antiquarian, Theodore Bent, to excavate the ruins. It was the kind of thinking that went into Rider Haggard's great romantic novels of Africa, *She* and *King Solomon's Mines*. Not for many years was the native origin of Zimbabwe to be both archaeologically proved and accepted.

DELOS

A Greek trading center

The rocky barren islet of Delos, a mere speck in the middle of the Aegean Sea, owed its importance largely to accidental factors. The mythical birthplace of the god Apollo, it became in Archaic Greek times the leading religious center of the Ionians and the home of splendid festivals held in the god's honor. Because of its religious importance it was chosen as the center of the naval confederacy, or "empire," which Athens built up after the defeat of the Persian invasion of Greece in 480–479 BC. In Hellenistic times it reached a peak of importance as a great trading center, especially after 166 BC when Rome, already arbiter of Greek affairs though not yet master of their country, backed Delos as a rival to Rhodes, which had long monopolized the commerce between the Near East and the Aegean. Both islands flourished on the transit trade, and from the mid-2nd to the early 1st century BC Delos became something of a boom city with a rapidly expanding, cosmopolitan population. It was a banking center, the major grain market for the Aegean and under the Romans a slave market which boasted sales as high as 10,000 slaves a day. The principal ruins on the island, including the residential quarter and many of the public buildings, date from this period. The visitor to Delos may be more intrigued by the far more ancient Archaic lions, by the sanctuary of Apollo, the venerable shrines on Mount Cynthus or the huge stone phalluses connected with the mystic rites of Dionysus. But it is the late Classical ruins which reflect the most interesting part of the island's long history. For in many respects, though not in all, Delos was a typical Hellenistic city.

There are historical periods which appeal to us because they are so different from our own. We admire, for example, the confidence, the purity, the high-mindedness of Classical Greece; or we are intrigued by the enduring but utterly alien civilization of ancient Egypt. But there are also periods which attract us because they seem so much like our own, and the Hellenistic age is one of these.

Perhaps it has been too much overshadowed by the achievements of Classical Greece on the one hand and of Rome on the other – though the Romans in great part merely consolidated what the Hellenes had begun. It opened with the astonishing conquests of Alexander the Great, who in a few years (334–323 BC) had conquered an empire of some 2 million square miles, stretching from Greece to India. It ended with the defeat of Cleopatra of Egypt by the Romans in 31 BC. Though Alexander's empire soon broke up into three main kingdoms – and Pergamum, in Asia Minor, a fourth, later on – nothing was ever the same again. The ruling classes all over the known world, whether Greek or not, became Hellenized; many new Hellenic cities were founded by Alexander and his successors, and some of these turned into huge metropolises, manned by hordes of bureaucrats and with populations in the hundreds of thousands. These cities were standardized and were if possible laid out in a grid pattern, like many today. People moved easily from city to city over the entire huge area; an international language, the Greek *koiné*, developed and trade routes were opened up which reached as far as the Baltic, Africa, Russia and even China. Industrial and economic activity was intense. The arts became internationalized, philosophy more skeptical, technology, science and scholarship as advanced as they would be until our day, with famous libraries at Alexandria in Egypt and at Pergamum. In short, it was an opulent, sophisticated, international civilization – a restless, seeking civilization much like our own.

The Greeks had created the first truly international world. Today we have Arabs in London and American business colonies in the Gulf states. Delos was little different. Among the merchants who lived or traded there were Greeks from all over the Mediterranean, Romans, Syrians, Phoenicians, Alexandrians, Arabs, and traders from Yemen and the Persian Gulf. Archaeologists have discovered that a dock system built at Delos about 130 BC was made of granite from Egypt. Many of the once magnificent public buildings, and others within the sanctuary of Apollo, were donated by Hellenistic monarchs. For example Queen Stratonice of the Seleucid kingdom (Syria and Mesopotamia) was an important benefactress of the sanctuary. There was a synagogue at Delos, for this was the period of the great Jewish Dispersion, and temples to Isis and Serapis, Egyptian gods who were now worshiped all over the Greco-Roman world from India to Italy. The old certainties and the local loyalties had broken down in this melting pot of a world and most of the old gods (but not Apollo) had died or had been absorbed into other deities from other nations. There was a multiplicity of sects, mysteries and philosophies emphasizing salvation and the private and personal rather than the public and impersonal of earlier times. Even astrology was much in vogue, as it is today.

The arts grew both more ornate and more realistic, expressing the restlessness of the age in a dynamic statue group like the famous Laocoön or its opulence in the mellow voluptuousness of the Venus de Milo. The new emphasis on the individual produced for the first time realistic portrait heads – and the newly rich merchants of Delos were not backward in having their features immortalized in stone busts. A more "modern" realism was also to be found in poetry and the drama, and the art of painting reached new heights of representation. Unfortunately little of the painting has survived, but the magnificent mosaics of Delos, in particular the one showing Dionysus riding a leopard, give the visitor a good idea of what these paintings must have been like.

Delos' prosperity was short-lived. From arbiter of Greek affairs Rome became the conqueror, and during the wars between Rome and Mithridates of Pontus (88 and 69 BC) Delos was twice sacked. Its ruin was completed by the economic competition of Italian ports like Puteoli. From a flourishing city Delos declined to little more than a village. Today the island is uninhabited for most of the year, but has become, quite deservedly, a major tourist attraction.

With its narrow streets and small size, Delos was no planned city, no metropolis; but in other respects its ruins can tell us much about that cosmopolitan period, the Hellenistic age.

Above right Archaic stone lion, one of a terrace of such lions dating from the late 7th century BC. There were perhaps 16 of them, carved in marble from the nearby island of Naxos. One now stands in Venice.

Right Arches over a water cistern near the theater. As Delos had only one stream, most of the city was dependent on wells and cisterns for its water supply. The paving which rested on the arches has now disappeared.

Far right The remains of the Serapeion, the sanctuary of the Egyptian god Serapis, who enjoyed a great vogue in the Hellenistic Greek world. In the background the standing columns are what remain of the temple dedicated to Serapis' consort Isis.

Above The stump of a gigantic phallus, from the shrine of Dionysus near the sanctuary of Apollo. These phalluses played an important part in the mystic fertility rites of Dionysus.

Left Statues of one Cleopatra (a common name) and her husband in the ruins of their once elegant house. At the base of the statues is the following inscription: "Cleopatra, daughter of Adrastus of Myrrhinus, [has set up the statue of] her husband Dioscurides, son of Theodorus of Myrrhinus, who dedicated the two silver tripods on either side of the entrance to the temple of Apollo at Delphi."

Top left The remains of the Establishment of the Poseidoniasts of Berytus. The foreign merchants who came to Delos tended to form national and professional associations, often under the patronage of a national deity. These varied buildings belonged to the association of merchants from Berytus (now Beirut in Lebanon) under the protection of the god Poseidon of Berytus.

Above left This whimsical statue of Pan and Aphrodite was found in the Establishment of the Poseidoniasts of Berytus (it is now in the National Museum, Athens). The horned goat-god is making advances to Aphrodite, who half-heartedly tries to fend him off with a slipper. A winged Cupid, symbolizing love, flies between them.

Top The House of the Hermes, as it survives today, and as reconstructed by an artist (**above**). The house was terraced up a hillside and had four stories of which three are partly preserved. The central courtyard was framed by colonnades on two levels. Though Greek in style, these airy, comfortable houses were built by resident merchants of many nations who made their fortunes in trade. The artist's impression shows the inner courtyard as it might have looked in the 2nd century BC. The grander houses of Delos were decorated inside with mosaics on the floors of the principal rooms.

Opposite above Mosaic of Dionysus riding a leopard, from the House of the Masks. The mosaics of Delos, reflecting Hellenistic painting, are among the finest to have survived from the period.

Opposite below Detail of another fine mosaic in the House of the Dolphins (named after the mosaic). The dolphins are ridden by a tiny cupid. The artist was Asclepiades of Aradus (in Phoenicia).

ANGKOR

Capital of ancient Cambodia

Angkor was long a fascinating mystery to Westerners. This vast city, crumbling and lost in the devouring jungles of Cambodia, had once been the center of the huge empire of the Khmers which rose and fell between the 9th and 15th centuries AD and occupied the greater part of Indochina. Not only had this empire been the most powerful in all of Southeast Asia but it had seen the most splendid flowering of Hindu art in the entire area. The city of Angkor itself once had a population of a million, but eventually it was deserted and forgotten, until in 1861 Henri Mouhot, a French naturalist, reached the site and published glowing accounts of it in the West. Subsequent French investigation of the remains of Angkor only increased the mystery, for the ruins turned out to be those of the largest complete city complex ever created by man before modern times. How was this possible? Even today excavation is by no means complete, and with Kampuchea (Cambodia) in continuing political turmoil, the jungle may again claim its prey.

Nevertheless much has been learned in recent years about this astonishing city. Angkor's vast buildings, with upturned gable ends and multiple towers on rising terraces, reach towards the Hindu heaven and are covered with sculpture and literally miles of stone-cut reliefs. The shrine of Angkor Wat, the crowning achievement of Khmer architecture, was built in the early 12th century, and with its symmetrical plan, intricate ornamentation and five great lotus towers it is the largest religious building in the world, larger than Vatican City as a whole. Nearby Angkor Thom, the royal city proper, begun about 1200, was surrounded by a wide moat and a wall 10 miles long with five gates, each 60 feet high. Inside were other shrines, including the Bayon, a royal temple, a grand plaza, and lakes, palaces and the houses and offices of the court, mostly built of wood and now gone. Outside were many other shrines and two huge reservoirs called *barays*.

Opposite The gate of the isolated Ta Som shrine, with the roots of a giant tree threatening to strangle it. Ta Som, situated in the northeast corner of the site, was one of the many smaller shrines at Angkor.

What strikes one about Angkor is the sheer size and power of the buildings, while the art, particularly the decoration and reliefs, seems to be in constant, restless motion. Tendrils and leaves twist nervously in intricate designs; animals cavort and tumble; in the narrative friezes people dance, cook, urge on a cockfight, or soldiers struggle in crowded combat while elephants rear, the enemy is trampled, slaves are captured. All is larger than life, agitated, frenetic – except for the quietly elegant celestial beauties known as *apsaras* or an occasional Buddha or other free-standing figure. Angkor either attracts or repels; but no one can remain indifferent to the message of these ruins: the Khmer were a dynamic, violent, cruel yet gifted people. Indeed their huge temples were built on the bodies of hordes of miserable slaves and peasants who toiled and died to celebrate the vanity of a race of god-kings. At Angkor's height the Khmers were the terror and glory of all Southeast Asia. Their armies included a corps of 200,000 war elephants, the cavalry and infantry were armed with rockets, catapults and cross-bows, and there was a navy of ships and armored canoes. The ruling classes loved war, luxury and pageantry and their life was a round of banqueting and processions, with much drug taking. They ate off gold and silver services, drank quantities of wine and sported in pleasure pools. Towers and statues in the capital glittered with gold; in the king's palace were 5,000 concubines and a bodyguard of tall amazons carrying lances and shields. Supporting the rulers and the topheavy bureaucracy were the innumerable slaves, most families owning from 10 to 100 each. The slaves also carried out the endless, backbreaking job of building ever larger temples, for the Khmers were profoundly religious and temples dominated the city. To maintain one temple required 306,372 servants who consumed 38,000 tons of rice a year.

How was this possible? What lay behind this wealth and luxury, this mania for building on a scale only exceeded by that of the Egyptian pyramids? First was the fantastic fertility of the Mekong river area, among the richest in the world. It produced inexhaustible supplies of fish and,

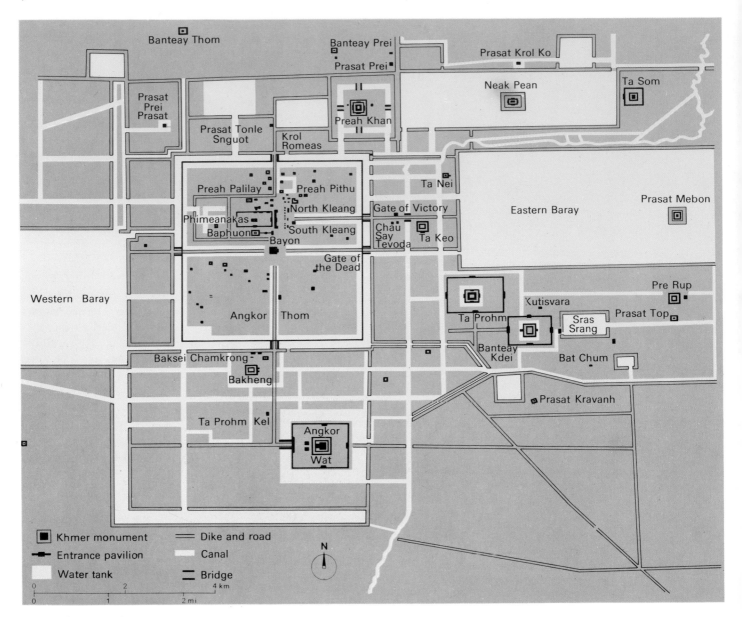

Banteay Thom
Banteay Prei
Prasat Prei
Prasat Krol Ko
Neak Pean
Ta Som
Prasat
Prei
Prasat
Prasat Tonle
Snguot
Krol
Romeas
Preah Khan
Ta Nei
Preah Palilay
Preah Pithu
Gate of Victory
Eastern Baray
Prasat Mebon
North Kleang
Phimeanakas
South Kleang
Chau
Say
Tevoda
Ta Keo
Baphuon
Bayon
Gate of
the Dead
Western Baray
Pre Rup
Kutisvara
Angkor Thom
Ta Prohm
Prasat Top
Sras
Srang
Baksei Chamkrong
Banteay
Kdei
Bat Chum
Bakheng
Prasat Kravanh
Ta Prohm Kel
Angkor
Wat

■ Khmer monument   —— Dike and road
█■ Entrance pavilion   ▢ Canal
▢ Water tank   ═ Bridge

N

0   2   4 km
0   1   2 mi

when irrigated, up to three crops of rice a year. There were animals to hunt, cotton to pick, precious woods in the northern forests and an abundance of iron ore and stone. From the predecessor empires of Funan and Chen-la the Khmers inherited a knowledge of agricultural hydraulics and land reclamation which they greatly developed, putting the slaves and peasants to work building water works all over the country and especially in and around Angkor, where the two huge *barays* supplied a network of canals, pipelines and channels to irrigate the growing areas in the drier seasons. The canals, also used for transportation, were supplemented by a network of paved roads. Angkor itself was one huge hydraulic system (see plan above) and its life-giving water was under the control of the king, the intermediary between the gods, givers of the water, and the earth, producer of wealth. Thus the capital was a sacred city. The potent influence of Indian culture and religion came also from Funan and Chen-la and the

Indian connection continued throughout the life of the empire. Finally there was the cult of the god-king, or Devaraja, the king equated with Shiva, Vishnu, and even Buddha. Each king would build his own temple mountain as a link with the gods on high and as his shrine after death, and each tried to build higher and larger than his predecessor. It was this powerful religious competition, backed by immense wealth, that led to the improbable grandeur of Angkor and eventually to its downfall. The extravagance of the kings proved too much for even the immense resources of the kingdom; an unparalleled frenzy for building seized the last great king, Jayavarman VII, who was responsible not only for Angkor Thom and the Bayon, but for many other shrines, over 100 hospitals and 150 rest houses. There were reverses, the waterworks silted up, and Angkor was finally abandoned in the 15th century – though the monarchy lingered on, a shadow of its former self, until 1970.

Above Ta Keo, dated about 1020 AD, was the first of the royal temples to be built entirely of stone. The building forms a square with sides 450 feet long – small by Angkor standards. These huge structures were called "temple mountains" because they were built upward on terraces to bring their royal owners in touch with the gods on high.

Right A view along the magnificent second terrace of Angkor Wat. Behind this facade was a library.

Opposite The city of Angkor was laid out on a grid of canals, channels and the two huge raised *barays* or reservoirs, all designed to irrigate the surrounding area. The wealth thus produced from crops went largely into the building of one royal shrine after another, most of which, including the famous Angkor Wat and the Bayon, at the heart of the royal city of Angkor Thom, are indicated.

Left Angkor Wat, seen here across the moat, is the largest individual structure in Angkor and one of the largest in the world. It is Suryavarman II's personal temple mountain, palace and mortuary shrine. Built after 1113 AD, it is 1,700 yards long and 1,550 wide and is surrounded by a vast external cloister. Beyond that are almost four miles of lined moat, which also acted as a water supply. It opens to the west along a magnificent causeway lined with balustrades in the form of colossal serpents. The western gate complex is nearly as large as the principal shrines.

Above A magnificent flight of steps at the heart of Angkor Wat leads up to the summit of the mystical mountain, topped by its five lotus-bud towers. There are three principal enclosed terraces rising one above another toward the central Shiva shrine, the whole symbolizing the hub of the universe. It took 30 to 40 years to build the Wat, and as much stone was used in its construction as in the Great Pyramid in ancient Egypt – and all of this stone was carefully dressed and ornamented, much of it *in situ* after the building's erection.

Left A good impression of the sheer size and complexity of Angkor Wat can be gained from this aerial photograph.

Left One of the gateways to the walled city of Angkor Thom, built about 1200 AD by Jayavarman VII, the last great Khmer king. The complex included the existing Phimeanakas, the ancient palace of the kings, as well as a number of earlier shrines, and Jayavarman's own temple mountain, the Bayon. The gateways and the many towers of the Bayon all displayed colossal, four-ways-looking masks of the Bodhisattva, the Buddhist king's patron deity.

Above The causeway, entering Angkor Thom over its surrounding moat, is bordered by a mile-long balustrade of squatting gods. They are pulling on the body of the cosmic snake, using it to churn, in Hindu mythology, the worlds like butter out of the originating ocean of milk.

Left The lake shrine of Neak Pean was one of the many religious buildings put up by Jayavarman VII, whose city was the Thom and whose temple mountain was the Bayon within it. Jayavarman adopted Buddhism as his state religion. He died in 1219, a very old man, after 30-odd years of warfare and feverish building.

Above Banteay Srei, a private, non-royal shrine lying 12 miles north of Angkor, is one of the loveliest and earliest (967 AD) of all. The inventive and elaborate style of Banteay Srei is shown in the large freestanding statue of a monkey (**left**), in one of the *apsaras* (heavenly girls) (**center**) and in the intricate gable relief (**right**) which illustrates a Hindu legend about Shiva, especially associated with mountains. The god is shown with his wife seated on Mount Kailasha, quieting the demon Ravana with the touch of a foot.

Right Relief sculpture at Angkor Wat, showing a battle between the Khmer and their enemy, the Cham. The open colonnaded gallery on the first story of the Wat contains over a mile of such sculpture, some six feet high, and originally painted and gilded. The artists at Angkor Wat were especially gifted in relief sculpture, its movement often reminiscent of the dance as it still exists in Thailand, Burma and Indonesia. In relief only some half-inch deep the artists have represented a complex world of mingled myth and reality, based on Hindu legends as well as Khmer history, and full of life and movement.

Far right Celestial courtesans from Angkor Wat, known as *apsaras*. These stylized, recurrent figures add a welcome note of sensuous calm to the powerful, frenetic art of the Khmers. With their elaborate clothing, jewels and hairstyles, they represent the Khmer ideal of feminine beauty. Modeled on court or temple dancers, they also hint at the sophistication of Khmer court life.

MACHU PICCHU

An Inca fortress city

The Inca city of Machu Picchu presents an astonishing sight to those who are hardy enough to negotiate the single narrow stone road, sometimes stepped, that leads along the crest of the Andes to the city. Some 9,000 feet in elevation, Machu Picchu tops a narrow saddle of rock between two precipitous mountains, with sheer drops on either side and a defensive wall guarding the only approach from the south. Built probably in the 15th century AD, Machu Picchu served briefly as a refuge for fleeing Incas after the Spanish conquest in the 1530s but was then abandoned. Over 100 acres of stone buildings of fine Inca masonry, the granite blocks set closely together without mortar, exhibit the highly developed engineering skill of those who built the city. Impressive as it is, Machu Picchu was in its day a typical Inca provincial city. Its renown depends on the fact that it is by far the best-preserved Inca city left to us.

For centuries after the Spanish conquest Machu Picchu was totally forgotten until it was dramatically re-discovered in 1911 by the American explorer, Hiram Bingham. Since his day a great deal has been learned about the huge Inca empire, as well as about its sister Amerindian empire, the Aztec, in Mexico to the north, both of which were brutally destroyed at the height of their powers by a handful of Spanish conquistadors. Though the Spaniards had primitive guns and used horses, they did not possess a notably superior culture to that of their victims. Nevertheless only two years after Cortés landed on the Gulf of Mexico in 1519 the Aztec empire was in ruins.

It took somewhat longer to subdue the Incas. In 1531

Opposite above Machu Picchu, dramatically sited in the high Andes, is the most perfectly preserved Inca city in Peru.

Below Two sketches by Poma de Ayala (1584–1614) of Inca life shortly after the conquest. De Ayala was himself a native Inca. The *taclla* or foot plow (**left**), here being used during the June potato harvest, was an ancient agricultural tool of the high Andes. The *quipu*, a string counting device (**right**), was the Inca's only method of keeping numerical records. Though highly civilized, the Incas had no writing.

Francisco Pizarro, after a preliminary reconnaissance, captured Tumbes, a coastal town in Peru, and with only 62 horsemen and 102 foot soldiers marched boldly inland to meet the Inca emperor himself in order to claim Peru for Philip of Spain and to gain as much gold as he could get. He met Atahuallpa, the emperor, encamped with his army outside Cajamarca. When Atahuallpa visited the Spanish camp Pizarro seized him, and with this bold stroke the machinery of Inca government came to a halt and the demoralized Indians offered little further resistance. Atahuallpa himself attempted to appeal to the Spanish lust for gold by offering to fill a large room with gold and two others with silver. To find the metal he ordered two temples, one of them the great Sun Temple at Cuzco, the capital, to be stripped of their treasures, which the Spaniards then melted down. But to no avail. Eventually the emperor was murdered, and once the head of state was dead, the highly centralized Inca empire fell apart. Who can tell what might have happened if these vigorous Indian states had been allowed to develop on their own?

The Incas as well as the Aztecs were latecomers, virtually barbarian conquerors, who united under their sway numerous states whose cultural foundations dated back, in both areas, to around 1000 BC. Both empires were barely 100 years old when the Spaniards destroyed them, but the cultures upon which they were based were far older. In Mesoamerica the Olmecs of the Gulf coast created the first true civilization – at about the time of the biblical David and Solomon – but left little to remember them by except the huge, enigmatic heads they carved out of basalt boulders. Better known are the much later Maya, masters of astronomy, writing and arithmetic, whose sprawling ceremonial cities flourished in Guatemala to about 900 AD and then in Yucatan into perhaps the 13th century. In Mexico proper the impressive remains of the great pyramided city of Teotihuacan, destroyed about 750 AD, can still be seen today in the outskirts of Mexico City, once the Aztec capital.

The Inca empire had no less impressive antecedents in numerous earlier cities and states sited along the west coast of South America. During the so-called Classic Period, for instance (about 200 BC to 900 AD), six major nations dominated the area. Of these, the most powerful was the Mochica nation, whose astonishingly realistic effigy pots in the shape of people, animals, fish and plants reached a level of portrayal outstanding even today. The sophisticated Mochica irrigation works included canals and aqueducts, one of which was over 50 feet high, and their central temple, the Huaca del Sol was the largest mud-brick building in the prehispanic New World. It is estimated that over 130 million bricks went into it.

These were but two of the many predecessor states of the Inca empire. In the first half of the 15th century, for instance, the kingdom of Chimu, which supplanted that of Mochica, became one of the most powerful in the central Andes and a principal rival to the growing Inca state. The Incas themselves originally formed one of the smallest of the city states struggling in the southern Sierra for political power. One by one they subdued the neighboring states, and by the early 16th century they had conquered an empire 200 miles wide and 2,000 long over which they spread their own culture like a veneer on top of the diverse native traditions. A combination of good administration and communications with military power kept this huge empire in control. From his capital at Cuzco, with its massive stone palaces and Sun Temple resplendent with sheets of gold, the Sapa Inca or Emperor ruled as a god over his many provinces, all linked to the capital by an extensive network of roads. With no wheeled transport, messages were sent by runners and goods were carried by llamas or men. Numerical records, in the absence of true writing, were kept by a device of knotted strings called the *quipu*. Like the Romans, the Incas were great engineers as well as administrators, and when a new province was conquered it was first surveyed and then plans drawn up for new lands or land improvement schemes to augment the tribute quota. The tribute in turn went into the support of the court at Cuzco and the army.

In each province the focus of government was the Inca new town, like Machu Picchu, or former capitals like Chan Chan of the Chimus. Here the governor levied tribute and administered the water control, land improvement and irrigation projects that made the empire so fruitful. Machu Picchu has all the salient features of such a provincial city – a central plaza, flanked by the palace, the Sun Temple and various public buildings, a defensive wall, an efficient water system supplying numerous baths and fountains, and terraced hillsides for the intensive growing of crops.

Above right Trapezoidal stone doorways and windows were characteristic of the superb architectural engineering of the Incas. This doorway at Machu Picchu leads into a small room with trapezoidal niches. To this day Inca walls stand up to earthquakes better than later ones.

Left An *aryballus* pot of the type found in burial caves outside the city (those within the city all having been looted). The *aryballus* was a characteristic Inca pottery shape. Such pots were carried by a rope, which was passed through the two loop-shaped lower handles and secured to a projecting nubbin on the upper part.

Above An aerial view of Machu Picchu shows it spilling down a high ridge in the Andes, with the agricultural terracing to the left of the central plaza, and the Intihuatana Hill, topped by its temple, rising above it. On the near side of the plaza are the houses of the nobles, with the royal palace and Sun Temple at its further (left) end backing on to the city wall.

Above The Temple of the Intihuatana Hill with its stone altar and post, whose purpose is not known. However, the name means "place to which the sun is tied," and similar altars are found in other Inca centers, suggesting a connection with the rising of the sun at the June solstice, the beginning of the Inca ceremonial year.

Right The Temple of the Three Windows on the sacred plaza, standing on heavy foundations built up from the terrace below. When it was excavated no objects were found inside the building, but numerous potsherds were found in the central plaza below. This suggests that they had been thrown out of the windows as offerings to the gods.

Left A fine example of Inca polygonal masonry in Tampu Machay, another Inca town. Mortar was never used, and so close is the fit between these massive stones that, as has often been said, a knife cannot be inserted between them. The stones were prepared by patient pecking with stone mauls, then abrading and sanding for a fine finish.

Below left A view of the central plaza, looking north. The hill has been terraced, with natural outcrops of rock being incorporated into the stonework. Behind the terraces are nobles' houses, and at the far end of the plaza is the Acllahuasi, a sort of harem where the most attractive girls were housed. The girls acted as royal seamstresses and concubines and were eventually sacrificed.

Below The sacred plaza, lying to the west of the central plaza. Two temples, both open-fronted, face onto the sacred plaza as well as the priest's house (at the back, with one of its two doorways partly blocked), which was probably the dwelling of the high priest or his deputies. It is lined with niches and has a large stone bench on one side. The High Priest, always a close relative of the Inca, must have only rarely visited the city.

Left The so-called "ingenuity" group of residential buildings, so named by Hiram Bingham because of the "ingenious stonecutting." The block, which lies near one end of the central plaza, is enclosed within a wall with only one entrance, and within it each house is self-contained.

Below left A view from the city south across the main terraces (which probably belonged to the Inca) to a block of gabled houses, some reconstructed. The wooden-framed, thatch roofs of these buildings were lashed to stone pegs built into the masonry of the building itself. The walls of the superbly-built agricultural terraces were about 15 feet high, but their full height did not appear above the next terrace down. Topsoil was laboriously brought up the mountain by hand and laid on a gravel base to form the fields. The produce no doubt went to the Inca and his retainers.

Above The royal palace, situated in the foreground, at the southern end of the central plaza. It was used to house the Inca and his family or important officials when they visited the city. Immediately behind the palace are the Temple of the Sun and the largest of the baths.

Top Part of the city wall, showing the city gate built into a defensive salient. The city of Machu Picchu was a natural fortress, protected on three sides by steep slopes and a mountain and open only to the south, where the main road entered. Here was a defensive wall with a dry moat. The city gate was built into the wall at the top of the ridge.

Above One of the 16 baths at Machu Picchu, built of granite. The Incas were masters of water engineering both for irrigating the terraces and for domestic uses. A narrow conduit brought water into Machu Picchu, crossing the moat on a stone aqueduct, piercing the wall, then flowing down past the Sun Temple through a series of baths and fountains.

Right One of the numerous burial caves found inside and outside the city. They were natural fissures in the rock, often modified with masonry, as here. The mummies were laid in niches in the caves which were then sealed by a wall. The wall of this cave has been removed, probably by tomb robbers.

Opposite Llamas loiter on an Inca terrace near Machu Picchu, high above the Urubamba river.

UR OF THE CHALDEES

Early Mesopotamian civilization

"And Terah took Abram his son and Lot the son of Haran, his grandson, and Sarai, his daughter-in-law, his son Abram's wife, and they went forth together from Ur of the Chaldees to go into the land of Canaan . . ." The Old Testament echoes with memories of Mesopotamia – the Creation story, Noah and the Flood, the wanderings of Abraham, the conquering Assyrians, the Babylonian Exile. Ironically, when the explorers and archaeologists of the 19th and early 20th centuries began to uncover the biblical remains in Mesopotamia they worked roughly backwards in time – first the great Assyrian palaces in the north, then Babylonia to the south, and finally the buried cities of Sumer and Akkad in the desolate deserts at the head of the Persian Gulf. One of the most sensational of these digs was that of Ur, traditional birthplace of Abraham, carried out by Sir Leonard Woolley in the 1920s, with its Royal Cemetery dating from the Early Dynastic period (about 2500 BC), its flood levels deep in the mound suggesting the origin of Noah and his Ark, its well-preserved temple ziggurat much like the larger one at Babylon, now gone, which probably inspired the story of the Tower of Babel. Woolley's work at Ur was brilliant; but far more important was the fact that he and his colleagues of the interwar period built up a new picture of Sumer as the birthplace of the first civilization. It seemed that the first real cities, the first writing, the first use of the wheel – and the farming surpluses that made it all possible – appeared here about 3000 BC, earlier than any other known civilization.

But what is a city? Sheer size? And what is civilization? We have seen the magnificent civilization of the Incas, who had neither the wheel nor writing. The huge cities of the Maya were not cities in our sense but ceremonial centers. And size? Kathleen Kenyon, reexcavating Jericho on the Jordan in the 1950s, uncovered at the lowest levels a 10-acre city dating from about 8000 BC, a city of mud-brick houses surrounded by a massive, defensive wall of stone, a city apparently supported not by agriculture but by trade. By 6000 BC Çatal Hüyük in Turkey, another recent discovery, had grown into a sophisticated city covering 32 acres. In fact since World War II the archaeologists have completely upset the older theories of the rise of civilization in Sumer. Civilization, it now appears, was a more gradual process than realized: it began thousands of years earlier than previously thought, and took place – and the first cities arose – not in Sumer alone but in a broad belt stretching from Turkey to India. The civilization of Sumer itself is now seen as a culmination, not a beginning, of a 2,000-year long Protoliterate period (including the Ubaid and Uruk phases) which saw the first cities, the first temples and primitive writing, and a flowering of architecture and the arts comparable to, but on a smaller scale, than that of Sumer itself.

Nevertheless Sumer could still be called the first fully literate civilization and truly urbanized society. Though Woolley and his generation knew something already of Sumer's antecedents, their main preoccupation was Sumer itself. Woolley belonged to that group of British archaeologists before World War I which included T. E. Lawrence and Gertrude Bell. In 1922, when Miss Bell had just been appointed head of the Antiquities Service of the new state of Iraq, Woolley came to Mesopotamia. "Mr Woolley arrived on Sunday," Miss Bell wrote in November. "He is a first-class digger and an archaeologist after my own heart . . . they are going to dig Ur, no less, and are prepared to put in two years' work." As it happened, Woolley dug at Ur for 12 years, doing a magnificent job of recording and publishing. Though sponsored by the British Museum and the University of Pennsylvania, on at least one occasion he had to pass the hat around the British community in Baghdad to meet expenses. One unexpected bonus was the richness of the Royal Cemetery. The splendor of the objects found may be judged from the following pages. But there were also the

Opposite Statuette of a goat in a tree, some 20 inches high, found in the Great Death-Pit, a mass grave in the Royal Cemetery of Ur. Made of wood, covered in gold and silver leaf, lapis lazuli and shell, it was one of a matching pair. It is now in the British Museum, London.

gruesome remains of soldiers, guards, musicians, and oxen harnessed to their chariots, all drugged and buried alive with their king to serve him in the afterlife. But despite the discovery of this cult of human sacrifice, Woolley and his colleagues in southern Iraq had also brought to light rich details of a lively and sophisticated civilization.

The Sumerians were a practical people, more interested in trade than in conquest, though there was constant bickering among their city states. The land was rich when irrigated, but had few other resources, not even wood, so that widespread trade – west into Syria, south towards India and east into Persia – was essential for their survival, and so too was the busy production of luxury goods, of textiles and art objects to exchange for the stone, metal ores, timber and semi-precious minerals they required. Much of this activity was centered in each city's temple, the home of its local god; but here was no theocracy, since the temple was in itself an economic unit, holding land, slaves and artisans and financing trading ventures. Thus, inevitably, it was in the temple that writing originated,

first to keep the records and finally to blossom out into a rich literature like that of the Epic of Gilgamesh, which contains the earliest version of the Flood story. The earliest mathematics also evolved in Sumer, based on the number 60, like our clocks today, and the first law code was evolved about 2100 BC by Ur-Nammu, a king of Ur, to keep this complex society in order. Above all, the Sumerians seem to have been the world's first bureaucrats. For instance, tens of thousands of clay tablets, surviving from the late Ur III phase, recorded in minute detail everything that moved or was moved – gold, wool, sheep, reeds.

Sumer disappeared as a power about 2000 BC, when the mighty Ur III Empire was destroyed by her age-old enemy from the east, Elam. But Sumer's rich culture lived on in Mesopotamia for another 1,500 years through the succeeding states and empires of Babylonia and Assyria, and eventually made significant contributions to the achievements of the West on the one hand and the world of Islam on the other.

Above A lion-headed eagle, symbolizing one
of the thousands of gods of ancient Sumer,
was excavated at Ubaid, close to Ur. It is a
powerful example of Early Dynastic sculpture.
It probably formed the lintel over the doorway
of the temple of the god Ninhursag. The finds
at Ubaid compensated for the fact that many of
the important Early Dynastic buildings of Ur
had been destroyed.

Right A gold helmet, presumably
ceremonial, found in the richly furnished
grave at Ur of one Meskalamdug, who may
have been a noble. It appears to have had cloth
padding inside, which was secured through
the holes round the edge. The hair style
denoted high rank.

Left The ziggurat at Ur, built by Ur-Nammu,
king of Ur, about 2100 BC and restored 1,500
years later by Nabonidus, the last king of
Babylon. These temple mountains were
characteristic of Mesopotamia, and find an
echo in the Bible as "The Tower of Babel."
Apart from one at Susa, the ziggurat of Ur is
the best preserved of all. In its final version it
may have had five to seven stages, but
probably only three in the original.

Top This delightful milking scene, a stone-inlaid frieze, was another of the decorations of the temple of Ninhursag at Ubaid. As head of Iraq's Antiquities Service, Gertrude Bell had to select the objects from Ur and Ubaid to go to the Iraq Museum at Baghdad. She wrote: "I had to tell them that I must take the milking scene. It's unique, and it depicts the life of the country at an immensely early date . . . it broke Mr. Woolley's heart."

Above A stone bowl found at Ur, Late Uruk period (3500–3000 BC). It is decorated with bulls and ears of corn in high relief.

Right Among the treasures uncovered by Woolley in the Royal Cemetery at Ur were nine lyres and two harps. One of the lyres, restored, is shown here. It was found, together with two other lyres, in the Great Death-Pit which contained 74 skeletons. The lyre was made of wood covered by gold leaf, but over the centuries the wood had decayed. By a brilliant archaeologist's trick, Woolley recovered the original shape by pouring plaster into the hole left by the decay of the wood. Music and musicians seem to have held an honorable place in Sumerian society. Skeletons of court musicians were found among those buried in the Royal Cemetery.

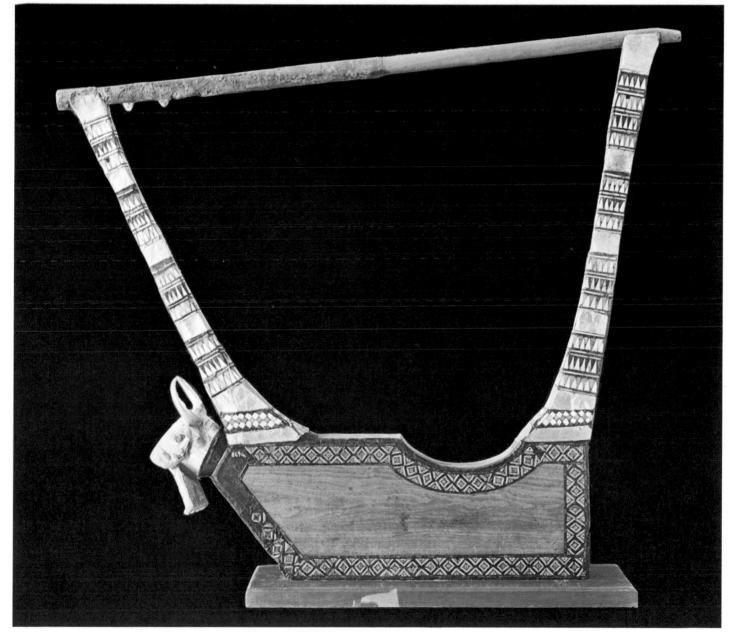

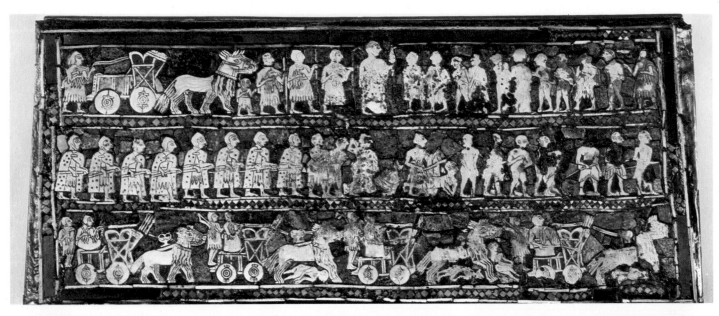

Above The enigmatic object known as the "Standard of Ur," made of wood inlaid with shell and lapis lazuli. It was found in a grave and must surely date from the time when Ur held the "Kingship of Sumer." On one side (top) is a battle scene. In the top two registers the king is standing before his solid-wheeled chariot while roped prisoners are brought before him; below are the chariots in action. They are pulled by pairs of small onagers, or wild asses. On the other side the king, in a fleeced skirt, is feasting, presumably to celebrate his victory. He is sitting with his companions (note the lyre-player to the right) while below him is a procession carrying either tribute or provisions for the feast.

Left An onager made of electrum ornaments a Sumerian double chariot ring from Ur. The Standard of Ur shows onagers and chariots with the reins passing through just such rings.

Above right One of the most exquisite of Woolley's finds was this solid gold dagger with its sheath in delicate filigree work. Sumer's active traders imported all the ores, precious stones and other materials used in such courtly products from distant points in Asia Minor, Afghanistan or the Persian Gulf. The skilled artisans who designed and made the objects were organized in craft unions and were much honored.

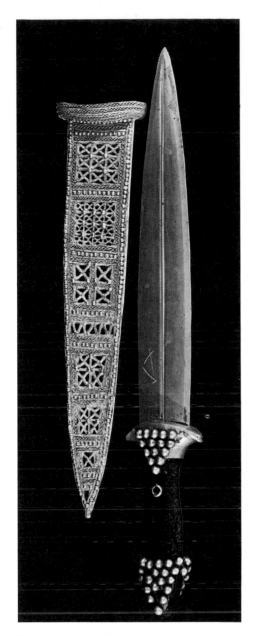

Top right An early clay tablet (about 2900 BC) from Jamdat Nasr lists areas of fields and crops. It is about 400 years older than the Royal Cemetery at Ur, and illustrates the origin of writing in record-keeping. The system of cuneiform writing was at the core of Mesopotamian civilization, and in such tablets even the most ephemeral records have been preserved. Many thousands of such clay tablets were found at Ur.

Right Cuneiform began in Uruk about 3100 BC with simple drawings of recognizable objects and numerals, then developed into a formalized system of writing used throughout the Near East. The first tablets were mere inventories. Later they began to record history as well, and finally a full-fledged literature.

THE EVOLUTION OF THE CUNEIFORM SIGNS

PICTOGRAMS		"CLASSICAL" SUMERIAN		OLD-AKKADIAN	OLD-ASSYRIAN	OLD-BABYLONIAN	NEO-ASSYRIAN	NEO-BABYLONIAN	Picture	Meaning
URUK UPRIGHT c.3100 BC	JEMDET NASR TURNED 90° TO LEFT c.2800 BC	LINEAR c.2400 BC	CUNEIFORM	c.2200 BC	c.1900 BC	c.1700 BC	c.700 BC	c.600 BC		
									NECK + HEAD	HEAD FRONT
									NECK+HEAD + BEARD or TEETH	MOUTH NOSE TOOTH VOICE SPEAK WORD
									SHROUDED BODY (?)	MAN
									SITTING BIRD	BIRD
									BULL'S HEAD	OX
									STAR	SKY HEAVEN-GOD GOD
									STREAM of WATER	WATER SEED FATHER SON
									LAND-PLOT + TREES	ORCHARD GREENERY TO GROW TO WRITE

PART TWO

Shrines and Temples

VEDUTA DEL CAST: D'ACROPOLIS DALLA PARTE DI TRAMONTANA

308

THE ACROPOLIS

The crowning glory of Athens

This holy citadel, this towering limestone platform, still dominates the plain of Athens. In the Bronze Age its narrow top, measuring only about 1,000 by 500 feet, held the entire town of Athens and the palace of its Mycenaean king. Always a center of worship as well as a natural fortress, by Classical times it had become a sanctuary of the gods, especially of the virgin goddess Athena. There were several earlier temples of Athena but the Acropolis as we know it today, as it was in Pericles' time in the 5th century BC, is still dominated by Athena's great temple, the Parthenon, now a ruined shell, that noble building whose Doric facade is echoed in countless banks, theaters and statehouses around the world. A hundred years after Pericles, the young Alexander of Macedon climbed the rock to dedicate a row of golden shields on the Parthenon to his victories. In 86 BC the tough Roman dictator Sulla stormed the Acropolis and ran off with the temple treasures. Visiting Athens, Mark Antony held nightly revels on the Acropolis and erected statues of himself and Cleopatra. Christianity came to the Acropolis much later, in Byzantine times, and the temple of the virgin Athena became a church of the Virgin Mary, which under the crusaders was converted to the Western rite as Notre Dame d'Athènes. Courtly French was now heard on the rock, and the singing of troubadours; and the Propylaea, the ancient monumental gateway, became an archbishop's palace – only to be turned into an elegant Renaissance palazzo by the Florentines. And everybody built walls and towers, including the Turks, who took over in 1458 and turned the Parthenon into a mosque, with a slender minaret. The Turkish commander of the fortress lived in the Propylaea and used the ancient Erechtheion for his harem.

Meantime, however, the Classical buildings had re-mained more or less intact, until in 1687 a well-placed mortar barrage – fired ironically enough by a Swedish field marshal, a lover of antiquity, who was employed by the besieging Venetians – ignited the powder stored by the Turks in the Parthenon and blew out its interior. In 1801–04 Lord Elgin, a British diplomat, removed most of the remaining sculptures and they may be seen in the British Museum today. Finally, after the Greek War of Independence (1821–32) the Acropolis was stripped of the accretions of centuries, a patriotic act, to reveal the ruins of the Periclean buildings much as we now know them.

The ghost of Periclean Athens haunts these ruins. In the long history of the Acropolis this one brief period – less than 50 years – stands out as an unparalleled achievement of human creativity that has never ceased to influence the course of Western civilization. Under Pericles, a guiding influence in the city for some 30 years until his death in 429 BC, Athens not only dominated Greece as "the school of Hellas," but set many precedents for the future. Hers was the first democracy, based on a respect for freedom and equality under the law; hers was the first drama, developed out of earlier Dionysiac rites. Significant advances were made in philosophy, mathematics and the writing of history, and a perfection was achieved in the arts and architecture that has never ceased to be admired and imitated. The Athenians knew they were living in great times and gloried in it. "Future ages will wonder at us," said Pericles, "as the present age wonders at us now." Yet these Athenians were human, after all, they were no saints, just as their temples and statues, once thought to have been classically white, were actually a riot of color – flesh tints and rouge on the marble statues and the buildings resplendent in blue, scarlet and gold. Their economy was based on slavery, though the slaves (except those in the silver mines) were relatively well treated. And they were unabashed imperialists. The Periclean Acropolis was paid for out of the tribute from their "allies," and when the little island of Melos refused to submit to them, they massacred every man on it. Nevertheless, they somehow achieved a delicate synthesis between boldness and

Opposite With its perfect proportions and commanding situation, the Parthenon—the temple of Athena on the Acropolis of Athens—is one of the most famous buildings in the world. Its interior was destroyed when a Turkish powder magazine blew up during the Venetian bombardment of 1687, as illustrated **below** in a contemporary Venetian engraving.

restraint, between the simplicity of the primitive and the elaboration of the sophisticated, between the forces of innovation and the virtues of tradition. Unfettered by religious creed or dogma, they were endlessly curious and richly creative, always making much out of little – the Classical ideal of restraint. "We are lovers of the beautiful," said Pericles, "yet with economy."

Such a fragile synthesis could not last; it soon fell apart under the blows of war, plague and the Macedonian conquest. But it is remarkable how much of the Periclean ideal was built into the Acropolis. Devastated by the Persians in 480 BC, the Acropolis lay in ruins until the 440s when under Pericles' guiding hand it was rebuilt, both as a memorial to the defeat of the Persians and as a showpiece of the Athenian ideal. The architecture was of the simplest: column and lintel, not far removed from the wooden prototype, but subtly refined in proportions. The sculpture displayed a characteristic Greek combination of restraint with exuberance, especially the masterly Panathenaea frieze in the Parthenon. The Greek drama, developed from one of the 50 or so religious festivals the Athenians enjoyed each year, was performed in the Theater of Dionysus at the base of the Acropolis. Near the theater was the Odeum of Pericles (now gone), devoted to competitions in music, central in Greek education.

Painting, too, was highly valued in Greece, though most of it has disappeared, and one wing of the Propylaea was an art gallery. Above all the Acropolis was primarily the shrine of Athena, and Athena *was* Athens. But to us perhaps the most characteristically Greek aspect of the Periclean Acropolis was the harmonious grouping of the buildings on the uneven rock, a triumph of order and proportion – and the fact that it belonged to and was used and loved by all the citizens of democratic Athens.

Below An artist's reconstruction of the Acropolis in the time of Pericles. The chief monuments are: **1** the Parthenon, the temple of Athena the virgin (Athena Parthenos), built 443–432 BC; **2** the Erechtheion (built 421–407 BC), a temple or shrine dedicated to Erechtheus, a mythical king of Athens, which also housed a number of other cults, including those of Athena and Poseidon; **3** the Propylaea, a monumental gateway (437–432 BC); **4** the temple of Athena the Victorious (Athena Nike, probably completed about 425 BC); **5** the colossal statue of Athena the Leader in Battle (Athena Promachos), made by Pheidias in the 450s to celebrate the victory over the Persians some 25 years previously. When the Persians attempted their second invasion of Greece in 480 BC, they destroyed the old Acropolis buildings and votive statues, but they were defeated at the Battle of Plataea the following year. The subsequent rebuilding of the Acropolis both celebrated the defeat of the Persians and symbolized Athenian domination of the Delian League, a confederacy set up originally to carry on the struggle against the Persians, but which became in effect an Athenian empire.

Left The Parthenon was designed by the famous Greek architect Ictinus, under the general direction of the sculptor Pheidias who was responsible for the overall scheme of reconstruction on the Acropolis. The structure is basically simple, consisting of a rectangle of Doric columns – 8 at each end and 17 down each side – supporting a shallow-angled roof. Inside were further colonnades and a cult room housing the majestic gold and ivory statue of Athena by Pheidias. What makes the Parthenon a great building is its perfect proportions, achieved by an extremely subtle calculation of optical effects, as can be seen in the photograph here; seen from a distance the temple platform looks level, but on close inspection it turns out to be very slightly curved. The architect knew that without that subtle curve the temple would look as if it sagged in the middle. Similarly, the Parthenon's columns were slightly narrowed (only 3/4 inch) toward their tops, again to avoid a spindly effect.

Below The Propylaea, the work of the architect Mnesicles, is one of the best-preserved buildings on the Acropolis. Designed as a monumental roofed gateway commanding the entrance to the Acropolis, its interior was richly decorated in blue and gold. Wall-paintings by Polygnotus and other famous artists were exhibited in a wing, the Pinacotheca. The plan of the Propylaea was several times altered, and it was never completed. In 1640 the building was damaged in another powder explosion under the Turks.

Overleaf A general view of the Acropolis, seen from the southwest, with the Parthenon overlooking the old defensive walls. To the left can be seen the small temple of Athena Nike built on a bastion in front of the Propylaea. In the central foreground are the substantial remains of the theater of Herodes Atticus, built in 161 AD by a wealthy Athenian and capable of holding 5,000 spectators.

Above One of the glories of the Parthenon was the sculptured frieze, parts of which were removed by Lord Elgin and are now in the British Museum. It ran high up around the cella on the inside of the building and must have been very difficult to see. The theme was the great Panathenaic procession of all the people which brought a new robe to the sacred wooden image of Athena. The two details here show sacrificial animals in the procession (top), who were followed by a group of elders in a relaxed mood (above).

Left and **right** Two fragments of the sculpture that once adorned the pediments at each end of the Parthenon. Now in the British Museum, they are all that survive of a tableau on the east pediment representing the birth of Athena, who sprang fully armed from the head of Zeus. The three figures on the left, usually called the "Three Fates," are thought to represent (left to right) the hearth-goddess Hestia, the sky-goddess Dione and the goddess of love Aphrodite. The reclining god on the right may be Dionysus, the god of wine and abandoned ecstasy.

Left The religious focus of the Parthenon and one of the most famous masterpieces of antiquity was Pheidias' imposing statue of Athena, some 40 feet high, which stood inside the temple. It has not survived, but copies have been identified from descriptions of it left by ancient authors. This Roman statuette of the 2nd century AD barely hints at the majesty and richness of ornamentation of the original, whose robes were of beaten gold and flesh parts of ivory. Athena wears a triple-crested helmet and in her right hand, supported by a column, she holds a figure of Victory. Her shield is by her side, along with the sacred snake, which was an emblem of the goddess.

Left Part of the Panathenaic frieze, still in its original position. With the roof keeping the light out in the time of Pericles, the frieze must have been in deep shadow and practically invisible from the ground, although originally, like all Greek sculpture, it was brightly painted. The panel shows a few of the superb horsemen in the procession, the best of which are in the British Museum.

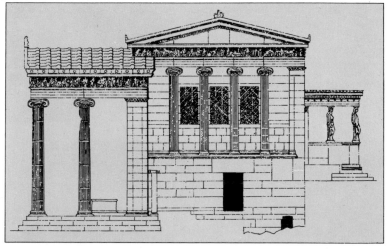

Above and **above right** The Erechtheion, an odd-shaped temple, is actually a brilliant compromise between different ground levels and the requirements of its various cults. It is built on an east-west axis, with the porch of maidens (the famous Caryatids) facing the Parthenon. The north porch has longer columns where the ground slopes away, as can be seen in the drawing (**right**) of the reconstructed west elevation. One of the existing Caryatids is a cast, the original being in the British Museum, and atmospheric pollution is now threatening serious damage to the remaining ones.

Opposite and **below** The small but exquisite temple of Athena Nike, goddess of victory, in the southwest corner of the Acropolis. It stands on a built-up platform overlooking the approach to the Propylaea. Its Ionic columns are surmounted by the original carved frieze. A detail, shown **below right**, depicts Greeks and Persians fighting (the Greek is on horseback).

THE MOSQUE OF SULTAN HASAN

A 14th-century mosque in Cairo

Cairo under the early Mamlūk sultans, who ruled Egypt and Syria during the 13th and 14th centuries AD, was a brilliant capital, a bustling commercial center, a city famous for its magnificent mosques, for its schools and its mausoleums, built and adorned in one of the last great flowerings of Muslim art and architecture. The sultans themselves, who ruled with an iron hand, were famous warriors, superb horsemen skilled in the use of the bow and the lance. They drove the last of the crusaders from the Holy Land and turned the Mongol hordes back from Egypt. As pious Muslims they were great builders too, and patrons of the arts who lived in luxurious splendor. Yet these sultans, the Mamlūks (the word means "owned" in Arabic), were actually descendants of slaves, mostly by origin Qipchāq Turks from the Volga steppes of Russia (and in a later Mamlūk dynasty, Circassian slaves), imported and trained to form an elite royal bodyguard, like the Turkish guards who dominated the last of the Abbasid Caliphs of Baghdad, or the famous Janissaries (Christian slaves from the Balkans) of the Ottoman empire. But the Mamlūks of Egypt, seizing power in the 1250s from the last of the descendants of Saladin, became sultans themselves; and thereafter a slave background continued to be the best qualification for gaining the sultanate, usually by craft or bloodshed. Consequently the average reign of the Mamlūks was only six years. Two of the greatest were the legendary Baybars, the real founder of Mamlūk power (ruled 1259–77), and Qalā'ūn (ruled 1279–93), who was so proud of his menial origin that he adopted the surname "thousander," referring to his exceptionally high price as a slave – 1,000 dinars. Qalā'ūn was the only Mamlūk whose line provided sultans for

several generations, but his descendants were all young when enthroned and became puppets in the hands of the emirs, their advisers. One of these descendants was Qalā'ūn's grandson Sultan Hasan, a minor ruler known only for his mosque. He came to the throne in 1347 at the age of 13, was deposed for three years by a jealous brother, and met a violent end in 1362.

Egypt under the Mamlūks, although ruled by a military dynasty of foreign slaves, was paradoxically a bastion of the older Arab culture in an Islamic world increasingly dominated by Turks and disrupted by the invading Mongols. Islam had come a long way since the armies of Muhammad and his successors had burst out of the Arabian desert in the 7th and 8th centuries to conquer an empire reaching from India to Spain. The religious and secular center of this empire, the Caliphate, moved first to Damascus and then, under the potent influence of Persian culture, to Baghdad. Here, under the Abbasids, was the golden age of Islam. It was brought to a brutal end in 1258 (just as the Mamlūk period was opening in Egypt) when the Mongols sacked Baghdad, destroying the Caliphate and ending the Arab domination of Islam, as well as any hope of a unified empire. Turkish tribes from the steppes had years earlier moved into the East and into Anatolia (Asia Minor) in the West, on the borders of Europe. Other Turks, like the slave guard Mamlūks, had infiltrated into the older centers of power. But despite this mixture of cultures and people, Islam itself survived and was strengthened, for Islam was a way of life, a simple and persuasive religion, a culture and a political system all in one, and its genius was to be able to absorb and transmute these differing elements into an enduring culture of its own. It was the Muslims who rediscovered, enlarged upon and transmitted to the West much of the philosophical and scientific learning of the Greeks, as well as the mathematics of India with its "arabic" numerals, and papermaking from China.

The relics of Islam's great days are to be found from Spain to India – the Alhambra, the mosques of Cairo or Istanbul, the exquisite Dome of the Rock in Jerusalem,

Opposite above The grandeur of the mosque of Sultan Hasan is conveyed in a 19th-century view by David Roberts, a popular illustrator of the eastern scene.

Below Words from the Koran in Kufic stylized script, part of the great stucco frieze decorating the *iwan* which faced towards Mecca in the mosque of Sultan Hasan. Islam brought the use of calligraphy as a decorative motif to a high art.

which is one of Islam's oldest monuments, the vast ruined mausoleum of Uljaitu in Persia or the palaces and mausoleums of the Moghuls in India. Most of the relics are standing monuments, for there has been comparatively little archaeological work in Islamic lands, and the majority are mosques, or mosque-like buildings like the *madrasas* or religious schools; for the mosque was the most distinctive form of Islamic architecture, and although individual mosques are as different as the national cultures out of which they arose, they all have common elements marking them as a product of Islam. The Islamic religion is a simple system of beliefs, duties and values, with no liturgy, sacraments or organized priesthood. The mosque therefore is primarily a place for communal prayer, open to all, with a large hushed courtyard where anybody can sit and relax, a covered sanctuary along one side for the worshipers, a niche, or *mihrab*, marking the direction of Mecca, a pulpit or *minbar* for the imam's Friday sermon, a fountain for ritual ablutions and a tall minaret for the call to prayer. Later refinements, of Persian origin, were the great arches, or *iwans*, on all four sides of the courtyard, the dome over the sanctuary, and finally an ornamental gate or porch. Otherwise the outside of the mosque was usually plain but inside it was highly decorated, either with

the brilliant faience tilework of the Persians or Turks, or the varicolored stone or marble panels of Cairo – but always in abstract patterns, for in Islam representational art was frowned upon, and there were no statues. Effective use was also made of superbly decorative calligraphy or writing, usually passages from the Koran.

The mosque of Sultan Hasan, despite its great size and its complex plan and decoration, exemplifies the same general pattern, but was the first in Cairo to incorporate a mausoleum. The Sultan's body never occupied his mausoleum however, for when Hasan was assassinated by rebellious Mamlūks in 1362, his mosque was unfinished. Begun in 1356, it was probably built on the foundations of the palace of an emir, which would account for its strangely irregular groundplan.

Below The southwest minaret, beside the mausoleum, the only original minaret still standing.

Below left The multicolored marble veneer paneling from the *mihrab* of the mosque, the arched niche marking the direction of Mecca. The use of thin veneer (resulting from a scarcity of marble) made the extraordinarily complicated patterns possible.

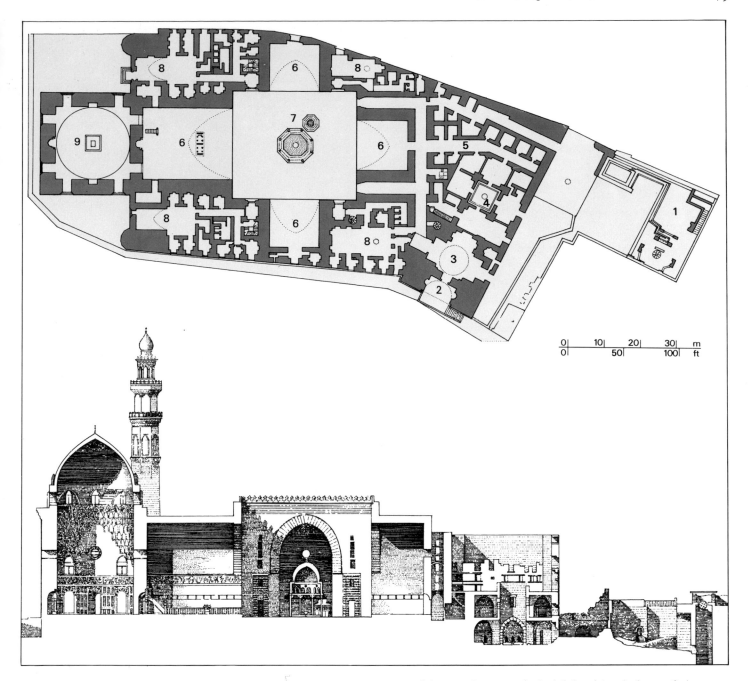

Above Ground plan and section of the mosque. **1** Water tower, part of a complex of buildings, all now in ruins, which included a market. **2** Grand entrance. **3** "Vestibule" or entrance-hall. **4** The ablution hall. **5** Corridor linking the "vestibule" with the mosque proper. **6** The four *iwans*, vast recessed arches arranged in a cruciform pattern around the central courtyard; the left-hand *iwan* is the one facing Mecca. **7** The central courtyard, with a pool under a domed canopy in the middle. **8** The four *madrasas*, or teaching schools, built in the spaces available behind the four corners of the main courtyard. **9** The great mausoleum built for but never occupied by Sultan Hasan.

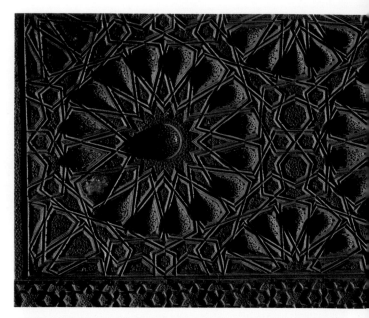

Top left An arched niche to the side of the grand entrance to the mosque. Note the intricate designs and decorative calligraphy at the top.

Top right A detail showing the superb abstract patterning of the original great bronze doors of the mosque. They are no longer in place, for in 1415 Sultan al-Mu'ayyad removed them to his own mosque-mausoleum at the Bab Zuwayla in Cairo.

Above The marble cenotaph in the mausoleum attached to the mosque. The mausoleum is a huge edifice with a dome 157 feet high, but the unfortunate Sultan Hasan never enjoyed repose in his own tomb, for he was killed by a rival faction and buried without honor.

Left One of the 200 lamps especially made for the mosque, of which 34 still survive. They were hung from the vaulted ceilings.

Right The spaciousness of the main courtyard and the great height of the four *iwans* flanking it can best be appreciated in another 19th-century engraving from Roberts.

Above The *mihrab*, the arched recess facing Mecca, inlaid with panels of green, yellow, red and pink marbles and porphyry. It is set in the rear wall of the *iwan* next to the mausoleum. To the right is the *minbar* or pulpit. The columns are of Crusader origin.

Above A medallion motif, part of a broad band of plaster stucco decoration running around the walls below the vaulted ceilings. The same motif occurs on the porch and the vestibule. The magnificent decoration of the mosque reflects the wealth and sophistication of Mamlūk Cairo.

STONEHENGE

Britain's great stone circle

The huge gray stones of the monument stand bleakly on the rolling uplands of the Salisbury Plain, much as they did 4,000 years ago. The sky here is open from horizon to horizon: one can see for miles; and all around these massive stones are the burial mounds of an ancient people. One feels instinctively that this place where land meets sky was once held to be sacred ground. But by whom? For what purpose? Stonehenge has been an enigma, and a famous one, for hundreds of years. "It stands as lonely in history," wrote Henry James, "as it does on the great plain." In the past it was attributed to the Danes, the Egyptians, the Phoenicians. Some insisted it was built by the people of Atlantis, others by the companions of King Arthur. According to Geoffrey of Monmouth, a 12th-century chronicler, the great magician Merlin, believing that "in these stones is a mystery ... not a stone is there that lacketh in virtue of witchcraft," brought them from Ireland by magic to stand over the graves of fallen British warriors. The more orderly 17th-century mind of Inigo Jones, who introduced Classical architecture into England, could only see in them the remains of a Roman temple. In the same century John Aubrey, and in the 18th century William Stukeley, fastened on the stones the most enduring myth of all, that Stonehenge was a Druid temple.

Curiously enough each generation pushed the supposed date of Stonehenge further back in time, from Geoffrey of Monmouth's 400 AD to Inigo Jones' Roman times, from Aubrey's 500 BC to estimates of recent years, when the first phase of the monument, based on radiocarbon dating, was confidently assigned to about 2200 BC and its final phase to perhaps 1300 BC, over a thousand years before the Druids. But in the 1960s even this dating was upset when it was discovered, by comparing radiocarbon dates with tree-ring sequences, that there was an increasing error as the

dates moved backward in time owing to variations in the amount of radiocarbon in the atmosphere at different times. Some scholars, led by Colin Renfrew of England, now maintain that the main stone "sarsen" structure of Stonehenge was built as early as around 2000 BC. And with this revision doubt has been cast on one of the pet beliefs of the older generation of archaeologists: that Stonehenge could never have been built by the rude barbarians of the time and therefore must have been constructed under the influence of the more advanced societies of the Aegean, perhaps even by wandering Mycenaean architects, who were masters at building in heavy "cyclopean" stone. The Mycenaeans, it is now suggested, were much too late.

Now we know that the major part of Stonehenge was the proud and independent creation of the Neolithic peoples of the West, as were the many other megalithic ("big stone") monuments all over Western Europe. And these stupendous works were earlier than any other similar monuments in the world. In Britain the precursors of Stonehenge were the so-called "causewayed camps" of the early Neolithic, circular earthworks with wide "causeways" leading into a series of sacred circles. These were undoubtedly tribal ceremonial centers. In later Neolithic times a number of huge "henge" monuments were built, circular bank-and-ditch enclosures with impressive timber halls inside them. It was at this time (perhaps 3000–2800 BC) that the original Stonehenge was laid out, a simple circular bank and ditch with a few stones. With the coming of the enterprising Beaker people from Europe in the Late Neolithic, more elaborate stone constructions appeared, notably the great stone circle at Avebury, which can still be seen. Stonehenge in period 2 now boasted a double crescent of so-called "bluestones" at its center. Finally, just into the Early Bronze Age (the Wessex period, around 2000 BC) the great circles of sarsen stones (period 3), whose ruins we now see, were erected at Stonehenge, with progressive refinements added to them well into the Bronze Age until work on the monument finally ceased about 1500 BC.

The labor that must have gone into the building of

Opposite The huge and mysterious stones of Stonehenge, standing isolated against the sky in one of the loneliest spots in southern Britain, have never ceased to capture the imagination and inspire conjectures about their origin and purpose. The aerial view (**below**), taken from the south, is less romantic but gives some impression of the setting on the wide plain.

Stonehenge, using the simplest tools and no metal, is astounding. The bluestones themselves were manhandled, partly by water, from far-off Wales, the huge sarsens were dragged from the Marlborough Downs 20 miles away. To move the heavier stones nearly a thousand men must have been needed, using hide ropes and rollers. The massive, seven-ton lintels were probably raised into position, little by little, on frameworks of timber. And all this was accomplished, it seems, by "barbarians who lacked even the use of metal," as Renfrew put it. How was it possible? Certainly no despotism was at work here, with whips and overseers; these monuments were built by whole communities, willingly working together – although it cannot be ruled out that one genius, a chief or a priest, was responsible for the work on Stonehenge 3, unique as it is. Paradoxically, the very fact that, as Renfrew suggests, Neolithic society was made up of simple, peaceful agricultural communities, with few ranks other than the chief and priest, made it all possible. Whole populations could be mobilized at a time, and once the labor was available the job itself was not as difficult as one might think, given time and effort. Later on, in the full Bronze Age, such mass mobilization would have been too difficult, for with metal weapons and increasing prosperity men were too busy fighting each other and vying for rank and privilege to carry out such massive tasks – and the building of megalithic monuments gradually ceased.

What impelled these Neolithic peasants to such tremendous efforts? The henges were obviously gathering places for whole communities, ceremonial centers – and perhaps something more. It had long been noted that Stonehenge was aligned on the rising of the midsummer sun, with the Heel Stone marking the position. In 1961 an American astronomer, using a computer, traced many other alignments in Stonehenge pointing to solar and lunar events, and it is now generally agreed that Stonehenge was a kind of observatory. But it was a temple too, sacred ground, for the livelihood of the Neolithic farmers depended upon the continued motions of the sun and moon, and at Stonehenge, it is believed, these were carefully observed and were probably invoked with impressive rites and ceremonies to ensure the orderly progress of nature. "In these stones is a mystery," said old Merlin. How right he was.

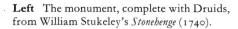

Left The monument, complete with Druids, from William Stukeley's *Stonehenge* (1740).

Right The three main building periods at Stonehenge covered many centuries. The first Stonehenge comprised the bank and ditch enclosure, the Heel Stone and the Aubrey holes, which never held any posts or stones. In the second period a double circle of bluestones was erected (the Q and R holes are the remains of this circle) and the Avenue leading northeast and then to the River Avon was built. In the active third period the bluestone circle was dismantled and over 80 enormous sarsen blocks were set up in the circle and trilithon we see today, as well as the four Station Stones (possibly astronomical markers) and the Slaughter Stone (part of a massive gateway). In the period 3B a bluestone oval was erected on the line of the present bluestone horseshoe, and the Y and Z holes were dug to receive the rest of the bluestones. But that project was abandoned; instead, in period 3C the bluestones were rearranged in the circle and horseshoe one can trace today.

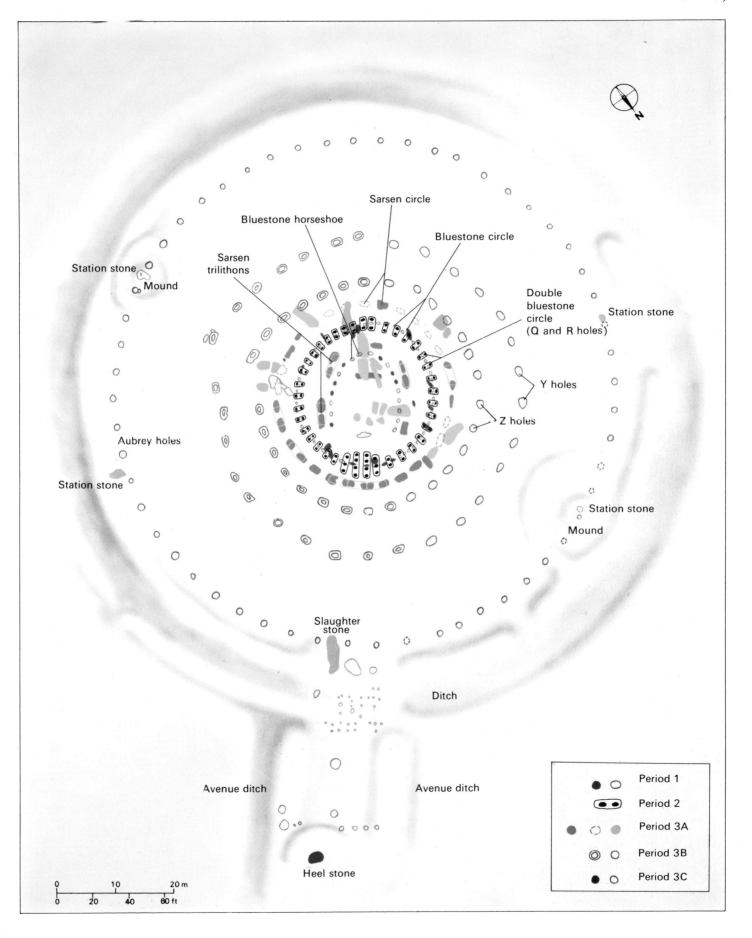

Sarsen circle

Bluestone horseshoe

Bluestone circle

Sarsen trilithons

Station stone

Mound

Double bluestone circle (Q and R holes)

Station stone

Y holes

Z holes

Aubrey holes

Station stone

Station stone

Mound

Slaughter stone

Ditch

Avenue ditch

Avenue ditch

Heel stone

		Period 1
		Period 2
		Period 3A
		Period 3B
		Period 3C

0 10 20 m

0 20 40 60 ft

Above right In this aerial view the outline of the original Stonehenge can be discerned, with its wide circular ditch and bank, still clearly visible, the Heel Stone outside the circle marking the summer solstice, and the 56 Aubrey holes or pits, named for the 17th-century antiquarian who first investigated them. About half have been excavated and are marked in white chalk. They may have had a ritual or even astronomical purpose. Intrusive cremation burials were found in many of them.

Right The main building phase of Stonehenge (period 3) can be clearly seen in this close-up aerial photograph. Its features include the circle of great sarsen stones with lintels (preserved almost intact to the right of the photograph), and the inner "horseshoe" of even larger sarsen stones. This was originally made up of five huge "trilithons," but only three now survive complete with their lintels. The remains of the circle and horseshoe of smaller bluestones may also be seen.

Far left The Heel Stone, part of the original Stonehenge. It marked, as it still does, the rising of the midsummer sun on the longest day of the year, as seen along the axis of the monument when standing at its center. The four Station Stones were placed at right angles to this axis.

Left The fallen lintel of one of the sarsen trilithons making up the horseshoe. The socket on the underside was made to fit the projecting tenon which can be seen on the upright stone still standing in the background.

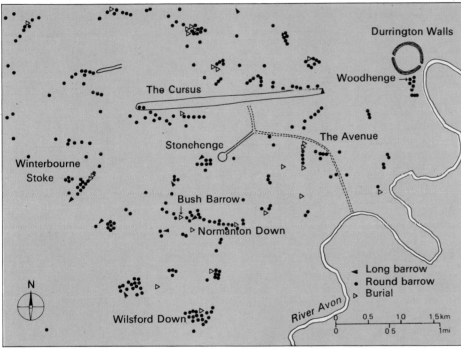

Left Stonehenge is in the middle of one of the richest archaeological areas in Britain. The whole of the chalk uplands comprising the Salisbury Plain and the Marlborough Downs is amazingly rich in ancient monuments, attesting to the ancient sanctity of the area over many centuries. The long barrows are Neolithic, the various types of round barrows, often grouped in "cemeteries," are Bronze Age. The Cursus was perhaps a ceremonial way. Two Neolithic ritual enclosures are also shown, and the Stonehenge Avenue leading to the Avon River, which may have been used to drag the bluestones from Wales from the river up to the monument.

Far left A close-up view of some of the great sarsen stones and lintels forming the main circle of Stonehenge. In the foreground the smaller stones are part of the bluestone circle that was one of the last additions to the site.

Left Representations of a dagger and an axe carved into one of the stones. Earlier scholars thought they could see in these the style of weapons made by the Mycenaean civilization in Greece (c. 1600–1300 BC). This was one of the chief arguments in favor of the theory (no longer generally accepted) that Stonehenge must have been built by visiting architects from the "advanced" civilizations of the Mediterranean basin.

HOUSES OF THE GODS

The temples of ancient Egypt

The ancient Egyptians, as their art confirms, were a cheerful and practical people, though of pervasive religious conviction. Despite the bewildering multiplicity of their gods, they always made sure that the chief gods at least had houses of their own in which they could be cared for and honored with the proper rituals. These were the temples, the "mansions of the gods," and the dead were also provided with houses, the elaborate stone-built tombs we are all familiar with; and not surprisingly, both temples and tombs were laid out on the same general plan as the house of the ordinary Egyptian, with an entranceway, a courtyard, a "living room" and a sanctuary or tomb chamber corresponding to the master's bedroom. But the house of the ordinary Egyptian was built of perishable mud-brick and wood, while the temples and tombs, because they were intended to last for eternity, were built of stone. It has been pointed out, and with some truth, that during Egypt's long history the gods with their temples, or the dead with their tombs, claimed a disproportionate share of Egypt's resources. The ancient Egyptians, however, would not have regarded this as wasteful; on the contrary they might well have boasted that their care in furnishing and maintaining the tombs and temples had ensured, as nothing else could, the stability and longevity of their civilization.

In a sense they may have been right. For the Egyptians were devoted to life – not to death, as is commonly thought. They hoped to live forever (they were the first people known to have formulated a concept of immortality), and they were convinced that life after death would go on much as it had before death if the old ways were strictly maintained with as little change as possible, if the gods continued to be honored with the correct rituals, and

above all if their kings, their pharaohs, who were half divine, half mortal, continued to carry out their role as mediators between gods and men. This was an essentially conservative philosophy and it undoubtedly helped to maintain this remarkable civilization for almost 3,000 years. If Egyptian society was conservative, however, it was never stagnant – except towards the end. In the New Kingdom period (c. 1567–1085 BC), for example, the Egyptians carved out a great overseas empire. But they also had their share of troubles – famine, foreign invasions, periods of near-anarchy – and consequently they thought of history as cyclical, the ebb and flow of good times and bad as the Nile floods and retreats each year. If disaster struck it was generally believed that neglect of the gods and of the principles of their ancestors was responsible. If the rituals and the worship were ever to cease, the Egyptians fully expected to see the end of their civilization as they knew it.

For the Egyptians the king was their link with the gods; he was responsible for everything in the country, he *was* Egypt. He owned the land, he was the law, he was the guarantor and transmitter of the divine order, for he alone, in theory at least, could communicate with the gods in their temples. The cultus temple was the house of a god where the king (or his deputy, the chief priest) could intercede with that god; but there was also another kind of temple, the mortuary temple, where the pharaoh himself after his death could receive the necessary worship and the funerary cult. For if the king, when alive, was the mediator between the gods and the people, his continued existence after death was considered necessary for the eternity of all the people, and this could only be ensured through the proper rituals in his temple.

The temples of both types that one sees in Egypt today date almost entirely from the New Kingdom dynasties and even later, through to the Ptolemaic period when Egypt was ruled by the successors of Alexander the Great, although the basic temple plan remained much the same throughout. Only traces of Old Kingdom temples remain (3rd millennium BC), and no complete Middle Kingdom temples (20th to 18th centuries BC) – because the New Kingdom pharaohs liked to rebuild them into their own larger edifices. But all showed much the same plan: a monumental gateway (the pylon) leading into an open, colonnaded court (which was as far as the ordinary people ever went), then a hall with rows of columns supporting the roof (the "reception room"), and finally the small, dark shrine of the resident god or pharaoh. Sometimes these elements were greatly elaborated, as at Karnak; but all the temples had one characteristic: they were processional ways leading towards the final holy of holies, the shrine. Here, three times a day, the king himself or the high priest reclothed and anointed the statue of the god and offered him food with elaborate rituals, censings and purifications. It was a ceremony of constant rebirth, of life continuing, considered essential for the peace and prosperity of the whole country.

These temples had no congregation; there was no communal worship. The priests were servants of the god, not of the community, and the influence of the temples was more secular than religious since the temples owned great estates and the more important ones were showered with gifts from the king. In fact the priests of Amun at Thebes became so powerful during the New Kingdom that a dynasty of high priests actually came to rule Upper Egypt. The populace did have some part in the rituals, however, for from time to time, during the great yearly festivals, the statue of the god was carried out from his temple in a colorful procession amid great popular rejoicing. For example, every year at the time of the Nile flood Amun was brought out from his shrine at Karnak and carried on a sacred barge up river to his other temple at Luxor, where he stayed for almost a month before being returned to his home. The people moreover could admire the exteriors of the great temples, even if they could not enter beyond the courtyards. The temples were originally painted inside and out in brilliant colors against a pure white background, the obelisks were tipped with gold, the statues and reliefs were brightly painted too, and the flagstaffs carried scarlet pennants. Thus in a manner quite strange to us, religion permeated and upheld Egyptian civilization. The continuity of 3,000 years attests to its validity.

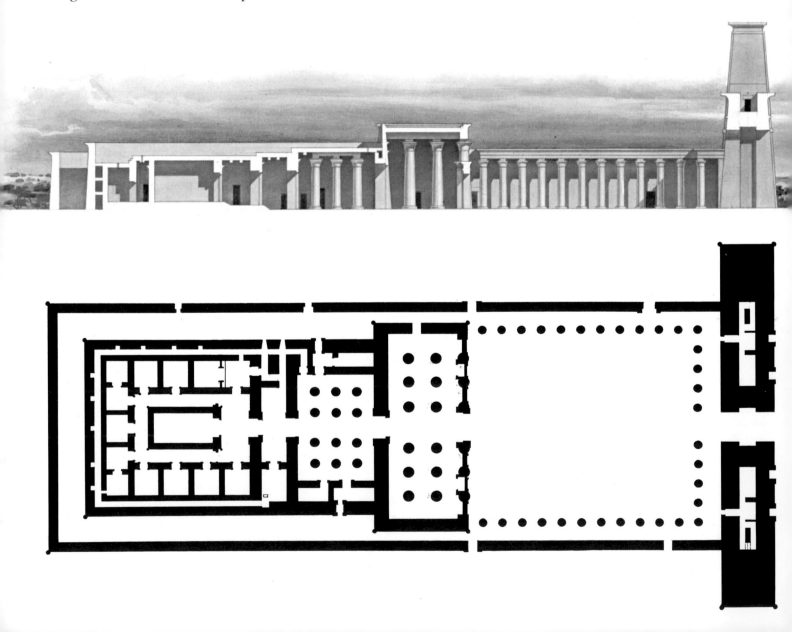

Opposite page Section and ground plan of the temple of Horus at Edfu, showing the plan of a typical Egyptian temple. The great pylon to the right opens into a wide court surrounded by a colonnade. The courtyard leads into a series of roofed halls supported by columns known as hypostyle halls. Beyond the halls is the inner sanctuary, the shrine of the god or pharaoh. As the "house" of the god, the temple followed the plan of a domestic dwelling, with its forecourt, reception rooms and private quarters at the rear. But a major temple like this would have had a large staff of priests, scribes, administrators, dancers and musicians, all ministering to the needs of the god.

Left That insatiable builder, Ramesses II (1290–1224 BC), added this huge pylon to the temple of Amun at Luxor (built by Amenophis III c. 1380), then placed in front of it no less than six gigantic statues of himself and two obelisks. Thebes had two temples of Amun, one at Luxor and the central one at Karnak.

Below The remains of one of the hypostyle halls of the temple at Luxor, with a double row of columns. The pylon and an obelisk can be seen in the background. The huge columns, topped by lotus capitals, derived from the slender, flower-topped reed columns of the primitive Egyptian temple.

QUEEN HATSHEPSUT'S MORTUARY TEMPLE
Queen Hatshepsut, who reigned between 1473 and 1458 BC, was a dominating character who ruled in her own right after the death of her husband and half-brother, Tuthmosis II. She built her mortuary temple in a dramatic setting (**left**) below the cliffs at Deir el-Bahri in the Valley of the Kings, a few miles west of Luxor. The temple, designed by the royal architect and favorite, Senenmut, was cut into the rock and surrounded by colonnades, which are seen in the photograph undergoing restoration. Its elegance is in pleasing contrast to the heavy work of Ramesses II. A view through part of the colonnade (**right**) shows some of the rich decoration on the inner walls. The best-known of these wall paintings depicts a naval expedition to the land of Punt (Somalia), whose members are seen returning in triumph (**below right**).

To the right of the entrance to Queen Hatshepsut's temple is a chapel dedicated to the underworld god Anubis (**below far left**). The god, to the left of the picture, is portrayed as a jackal. On the other side of the entrance is a chapel of Hathor, the goddess of music, love, fertility and dancing, whose head (**below left**) forms the capitals of the columns.

THE RAMESSEUM

One of the most imposing buildings at the edge of the
Valley of the Kings is the mortuary temple of the pharaoh
Ramesses II (1290–1224 BC). Its massive vulgarity contrasts
with the grace of Hatshepsut's earlier temple. Ramesses
commemorated his long reign by erecting huge temples and
colossal statues of himself from Memphis in the north to
Abu Simbel in the south (the famous rock-cut temple
recently moved to escape the waters of the Aswan dam).
The mortuary temple, known as the Ramesseum, is largely
in ruins, but the enormous columns of the hypostyle hall
(**above**) are still in part standing and supporting their roof.
Inside the western portal (**above right**) were four standing
column figures of the god Osiris, now decapitated. On the
ground beside them are the remains of a colossal statue of
Ramesses II, carved out of a single block of granite
weighing over 1,000 tons. It measures nearly 60 feet in
height (75 feet, including the crown) and is 22 feet broad
across the shoulders.

The walls of the Ramesseum are decorated with reliefs.
On the **left**, Ramesses II is portrayed in the thick of battle,
riding in his two-horse war chariot, while his enemies fall in
disarray beneath him. To the **right** the pharaoh is depicted
in his full dignity officiating at a sacrifice.

Above Another portrait of Ramesses II bringing a sacrifice of incense to the ancient Egyptian god Ptah, later identified with Osiris.

THE MORTUARY TEMPLE OF RAMESSES III

At Medinet Habu, less than a mile to the south of the Ramesseum, stands the impressive mortuary temple of a later pharaoh, Ramesses III (1184–1153 BC). There was already an earlier temple building on the site, and the original entrance to the temple complex (**left**) is now shut off. It consists of a high portal decorated with relief carving and crowned by a winged sun disk. (The two columns flanking the entrance were added in Ptolemaic times.) Behind the entrance is a courtyard (**below left**) whose walls are covered in decorative reliefs celebrating the life and triumphs of Ramesses III.

Above A black granite statue in the temple at Medinet Habu. It represents Sekhmet, the lion-headed goddess of the desert and of destruction, who was a special protector of the pharaoh.

Right The new entrance to the temple complex built by Ramesses III, known as the Pavilion. The reliefs depict Ramesses triumphing over his enemies. At his feet a prisoner begs for mercy.

Below A detail from the reliefs carved on the walls of the courtyard celebrating the pharaoh's campaigns abroad. It depicts bound Syrian captives being led before the pharaoh.

Below right Another relief at the entrance to the temple shows Ramesses III (the figure to the left) presenting prisoners to the gods Amun and Mut.

EGYPTIAN TEMPLE RITUAL

These paintings, decorating the walls of the temple of pharaoh Sethos I (1305–1290 BC) at Abydos, depict parts of the daily ritual carried out by the pharaoh or the high priest in the inner sanctuary. The sanctuary was the focus of the temple, where the cult image of the god was kept. The temple at Abydos was dedicated to the gods Amen-Re and Osiris. After prayers, purifications with incense and libations the image of Amen-Re was taken out of his shrine and his clothes and ointments were changed (**above**). In another part of the ritual, Osiris (**top right**, seated on a throne with Isis standing behind him) is offered a great collar · Later, back in his shrine and seated on a different throne

(**above**), Osiris is presented with implements symbolizing royalty: scepters, a flail, anklets and bracelets. Finally (**opposite**), the pharaoh offers Isis a plate of food. The food presented to the gods is then offered to a "King List" in another room, representing all the pharaohs or ancestors from the beginning, and is finally divided among the priests. This daily ritual thus ensures the well-being of the gods and a continuity with the past.

DELPHI

Sanctuary of Apollo

The Greeks believed that Delphi was the center of the world. According to legend Zeus released two eagles from the outer ends of the world and where they met, over Delphi , a stone called the Omphalos was placed to mark the spot. Certainly Delphi, with its famous oracle of Phoebus Apollo, was the religious center of the Greek world. Its magnificent site on the slopes of Mount Parnassus, which still inspires a sense of awe and mystery in the visitor, contributed to its fame, as did the Pythian games which were held every four years at Delphi, in the interval between the Olympian games. So great was the reputation of the oracle during its most splendid period in the 7th and 6th centuries BC that Greeks and foreigners from all over the Mediterranean sought its advice and approbation before embarking on any undertaking – waging war, founding a colony, contracting a marriage, framing laws or settling religious disputes. The Greek tyrants of Sicily showered Delphi with gifts and monuments, hoping to gain prestige in their homeland, and in the 6th century Croesus, the fabulously wealthy king of Lydia in Asia Minor, dedicated a famous golden treasure to the shrine. Croesus was encouraged to go to war against Cyrus of Persia when the oracle told him that if he did so a "mighty kingdom" would be destroyed. Unfortunately the kingdom proved to be his own. In fact Apollo's cryptic oracles were often open to several interpretations, because the priests of Delphi could not afford to offend any of their suppliants, whether tyrants or democrats, Greeks or foreigners. Nor were Delphi's "crooked and ambiguous utterances," as Aeschylus went so far as to call them, likely to discourage any state or individual intent upon carrying out a plan already decided upon. Sometimes the oracles were potentially disastrous. When the hosts of Xerxes the Persian closed in upon Athens, Delphi cravenly advised submission : "Flee to the ends of the earth. All is lost." But the Greeks courageously resisted the invader, and drove him off. This, and the oracle's flagrant favoring of Sparta against Athens during the Peloponnesian War (431–404 BC), cost it much prestige, ending its days of greatest influence.

Was it all a pretentious fraud? The Pythian priestess, a local woman of over 50, after drinking from a sacred spring and chewing a laurel leaf, mounted a tripod placed over a deep volcanic chasm in the inner shrine of Apollo's temple and became possessed of the god, uttering frenzied and incoherent cries which the priests interpreted as an oracle and released in hexameter verse. Yet these utterances must have been on the whole helpful or else the oracle could not have lasted for over a thousand years. Whatever the truth, Delphi did become, for many centuries, the adviser and conscience of the Greek world. It never sought riches, though by the 8th century it was already renowned for its wealth. It especially favored the arts, literature and philosophy and its shrine was adorned with works by all the great artists, sculptors and architects of the time. Pindar was its special poet, and Socrates, Plato and Aristotle all respected it. Socrates adapted one of the maxims carved on the temple, "Know thyself" (another was the very Greek "Nothing in excess") to his own purposes and was declared by the oracle to be "the wisest of men." Delphi was also the impartial and tolerant arbiter of all religious questions, great and small, preaching truth, inner purity and the power of the god to cleanse men from sin. It placed strong emphasis on the cult of heroes, and "canonized" many past worthies from all walks of life. And during the 7th and 6th centuries no leader of a colonial venture would embark without advice from Apollo on what site to choose or what god to worship. As a consequence, the priests of Delphi constituted a veritable intelligence bureau on the geography and politics of the Greek Mediterranean, and their pronouncements carried great weight. Above all, Delphi was a major force for cultural unity among the Greeks. Here Greeks from everywhere met, exchanged news and came to know one another, and again the priests benefited so that their oracles often revealed an astute appreciation of the

Opposite The temple of Apollo at Delphi, magnificently sited on the slopes of Mount Parnassus, home of the nine Muses. The temple was unusually long in order to accommodate the oracle within it.

problems presented to them. But they shied away from the hopeless task of promoting political unity among the Greeks.

Delphi's prestige rested in part upon its antiquity, for in late Mycenaean times (before 1100 BC) it appears to have been a shrine of Ge, the ancient earth goddess. Other cults succeeded, and finally the Greek god Apollo, as legend tells us, slew Ge's great snake, the Python, and seized the site for his oracle. The laurel of later times, the sacred spring, the vaporous chasm and the snake all suggest the earlier earth-worship, as does the site itself with its wild beauty, its towering cliffs, its dark and mysterious gorge and the frequent rumblings of the earth. Dionysus, the god of wine, of ecstasy, of divine madness later joined Apollo at Delphi. He was the perfect foil to the god of light, music, harmony and law, but was never anything but a junior partner, with no part in the oracle. In the 8th century Delphi was probably still a local shrine, but its growth as a Panhellenic center began in the 7th century

when the Amphictionic League, a religious association of many states, took control of the site. Under the Macedonians and then the Romans Delphi languished, though with periods of revival. In 67 AD the Emperor Nero is supposed to have helped himself to 500 of the best of Delphi's statues, but some 3,000 still remained when Pliny visited the site a few years later. In 390 AD Theodosius, in the name of Christianity, closed the oracle; 10 years later his successor, Arcadius, destroyed Apollo's temple. Thereafter the site became deeply buried and a village was built on top of it, which had to be removed before the French could begin in 1892 the excavations which revealed the ruins we see today. But the soul of Delphi had died long ago. When in 360 AD Julian the Apostate tried to consult the decrepit oracle, it answered: "Say to the King that the beautiful temple has fallen asunder, Phoebus no more has a sheltering roof nor a sacred cell; And the holy laurels are broken and wasted . . ."

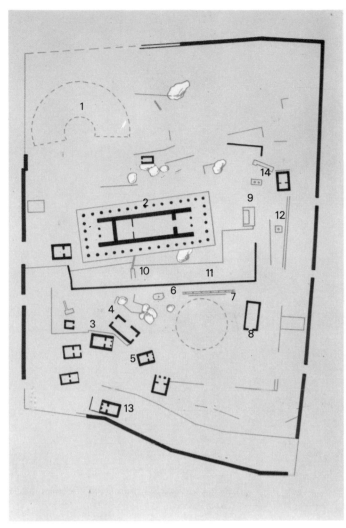

Left A plan of the sanctuary area at Delphi. **1** The Theater, first built in the 4th century BC, and rebuilt in Roman times. **2** The Temple of Apollo. **3** The Athenian Treasury, erected by the Athenians to house the treasure they dedicated to Apollo. By building such treasuries the Greek states hoped to enhance their prestige and influence the oracle in their favor. **4** The Bouleuterion, or council-chamber. **5** The Cnidian Treasury (Cnidos was a Greek city state in southwest Asia Minor). **6** The sphinx set up by the people of the island of Naxos. **7** The Stoa, a colonnade built by the Athenians. **8** The Corinthian Treasury, which housed the gold of Croesus. **9** Altar of Apollo. **10** Fountain. **11** The Polygonal Wall, a retaining wall made of polygonal stone blocks. **12** Tripod set up to commemorate the final victory over the Persians at Plataea in 479 BC. **13** The Treasury of the Siphnians (Siphnos is a small Aegean island). **14** Tripods dedicated by the tyrants of Syracuse in Sicily.

Opposite The few remaining columns of the Temple of Apollo. The temple was destroyed and rebuilt in the 6th century BC, and rebuilt once again after an earthquake in 373 BC.

Below An aerial view of Delphi as it is today, with the Sacred Way twisting steeply up through the Sanctuary. The Temple of Apollo, the Athenian Treasury and the Theater can be seen clearly. Above the Theater, partly cut into the rock of the sloping mountainside, is the Stadium where the athletic contests of the Pythian Games took place. It was built in the 5th century BC, but remodeled in Roman times, and could hold 7,000 spectators. The village of Kastri once occupied the site of Delphi but was moved down the road (it is visible in the background) to make way for the excavations.

Top The Treasury of the Athenians, restored in 1903–1906, was probably built in the 480s BC after the Battle of Marathon (490 BC). The carved reliefs depict the exploits of Hercules and Theseus.

Above The 6th-century BC Polygonal Wall, built to support the terrace of the Temple of Apollo. Its finely-fitted masonry blocks are covered with later inscriptions mainly recording the freeing of slaves. The slender columns in front of it are the remains of the Athenian Stoa, built to house trophies from the Persian Wars which ended in 479 BC.

Right The famous bronze Charioteer of Delphi, part of a chariot group, was discovered during the excavations. It was probably dedicated in 474 BC to commemorate the victory of the Sicilian prince Polyzelos in the chariot race at the Pythian Games. Its grace and nobility make it one of the finest of all Greek sculptures.

Opposite A short distance from the main site is a curious circular temple known as a *tholos*, built in the early 4th century BC. It was part of a group of buildings that formed the sanctuary of Athena Pronoia (Athena the Provident).

ARCHAIC SCULPTURE AT DELPHI

Top left Two archaic Greek statues of youths (*kouroi*), excavated at Delphi. They are among the earliest surviving *kouroi*, carved by an Argive in a powerful style which contrasts with the naturalism and grace of the later sculpture of the Classical period.

Left This historic photograph, taken in May, 1894, shows a group of archaeologists and workmen admiring the newly dug up torso of one of the archaic *kouroi* of the early 6th century BC.

Above A marble sphinx set on top of a 30-foot high column by the people of the island of Naxos about 570 BC. Why the Naxians chose to dedicate a sphinx to Apollo is not known, but they set up a similar sphinx on the island of Delos, also sacred to Apollo. The Naxians, with rich quarries, were pioneers in Greek marble sculpture.

THE TREASURY OF THE SIPHNIANS

The people of the small island of Siphnos, acquiring great wealth through their silver mines, built a magnificent marble treasury at Delphi in the 6th century BC. Shown **left** is one of the surviving fragments of the structure, a female column-figure (a caryatid), whose tall crown supported the roof of the porch, as shown in the artist's reconstruction **above**. The dignified and finely draped figure is a noble example of the caryatid type, which is best known from the six caryatids on the Acropolis of Athens (see above, p. 74). Part of the sculptured frieze of the Treasury also survives (**top**). The scene shown here depicts the battle of the gods and the giants. Cybele (the goddess of frenzy) and Hercules are in a chariot drawn by lions (one of which is attacking a warrior), while the two figures to the right represent Apollo and Artemis.

PART THREE

The Celebration of Kings

PERSEPOLIS

Ceremonial center of ancient Persia

The approach to Persepolis today, as in the past, lies across the high plateau country of central Persia (now Iran) with its bracing air, its huge craggy mountains and wide plains. Crossing one such plain the visitor sees, abruptly, set against a mountain, the great stone platform built by the kings of ancient Persia, dominated by the tall columns of Darius' Audience Hall and the heavy stone door- and window-frames of the palaces. Here was the ceremonial center, the sacred royal city of the Persian Empire. The architecture, like the landscape in which it is set, is monumental, imperial. In daylight its stones are somber gray, but if the visitor approaches at dusk they may glow in shifting tones of red as if the ancient structures, as one scholar has written, were once again "engulfed by the flames of long ago" set by Alexander the Great. For Alexander, the incomparable general, driving to the heart of the empire after twice defeating Darius III, also crossed this wide plain. It was January 31, 330 BC. Mounting the broad double stairway to the platform, he inspected the great Audience Hall, the palaces of the kings, Xerxes' Throne Hall with its 100 cedar columns, and the Treasury, filled with unimaginable wealth. Everywhere were rich hangings, tall bronze and gold-plated doors and processional stone friezes of courtiers and tribute-bearers seeming almost alive in their bright colors and ordered movement.

More and more Alexander had been hoping to inherit the mantle of the Great Kings as overlord in Asia. Nevertheless, urging his soldiers to avenge the Persians' earlier invasion of Greece, he loosed them on this shrine of Persia in an orgy of plundering and looting. Then in May he burned Persepolis. Different reasons have been given for this deed. One version has it that Alexander, as was his wont, got drunk one night at a feast. Urged on by Thaïs, a lovely Athenian courtesan, he led a tipsy garlanded procession, accompanied by the shrilling of flutes, to the Throne Hall where they threw in their torches. The flames spread quickly to other buildings. The destruction of Persepolis (though Alexander may have regretted it) and the subsequent murder of Darius III marked the end of the greatest empire of its time.

The empire endured for over 200 years. It was founded by the Persian Cyrus the Great, an able ruler who overthrew a previous empire of the Medes, fellow Aryans, in 553 BC. Thereafter he and his successors, in close union with the Medes, conquered an empire which at its greatest extent stretched from India to the borders of Greece and from Samarkand in Asia to Egypt. It was ruled by the Great King, whose person was surrounded by pomp and ritual and whose word was law; nevertheless it was far less harsh in its rule than the empires of its predecessors, the Assyrians and Babylonians. It was organized in 20 or so satrapies, or provinces, mostly of subject peoples who were fairly taxed and were treated with justice. Indeed the justice and tolerance of the Great Kings, such as Cyrus, who freed the Jews from their Babylonian captivity, was widely celebrated. Persian youths, it was said, were taught just three things: to ride, to draw the bow, and to speak the truth; and in one of his inscriptions Darius I (ruled 521–486 BC) wrote: "To that which is just, I am a friend, to that which is unjust I am no friend." The empire was ably administered, with an efficient, "pony express" courier service running over a network of good roads (one ran 1,500 miles from Sardis to Susa), banking facilities, an accepted coinage in the west, and a flourishing trade. The rulers of this multi-national empire, though despots, were cosmopolitan in outlook, feeling that it was their mission to bring order to all the peoples of their world. Their attempt to subdue Greece, however, failed; the first invasion was repulsed at the battle of Marathon in 490 BC, and the second at Salamis and Plataea 10–11 years later.

Persepolis, the ritual center where the kings were buried and the great ceremonies took place, was little known to

Opposite above The immense columns of the Audience Hall, or Apadana, the largest of the ceremonial buildings on the great terrace of Persepolis, begun by Darius I about 520 BC and completed by his son Xerxes and grandson Artaxerxes.

Below This magnificent double-headed lion-like beast formed the capital atop one of the Apadana's columns.

the Greeks until Alexander. It was built, from about 520 BC, by Darius I and his son and grandson, Xerxes (ruled 486–465 BC) and Artaxerxes (ruled 464–424 BC). Everything about it was monumental. The great terrace, rising some 40 to 50 feet above the plain, measured 1,400 by nearly 1,000 feet. It was originally ringed by a massive mud-brick defensive wall and below it, on the plain, were the residences of the courtiers. There were nine principal structures on the terrace, each walled in mud-brick and roofed with cedar beams. The largest was the great Audience Hall, or Apadana, with walls some 17 feet thick and inside a magnificent forest of 72 slender columns, each 65 feet high and topped by heavy bull-headed capitals (only 13 remain standing today). The plastered walls, the huge cedar roof beams and the stone reliefs would have been brightly painted and decorated, and the walls inside hung with richly embroidered tapestries or (to quote the words of the Book of Esther, describing the palace at Susa) "hangings of white cloth, of green and of blue, fastened with cords of fine linen and purple ..." The Apadana could have held up to 10,000 people.

It was this opulent assembly of buildings that Alexander burned in 330 BC. But in the end it was the Persians who might be said to have taught Alexander a lesson, for they had introduced him to a new idea, the idea of a world empire based on a fusion of peoples and cultures. Later on Alexander symbolically publicized his conversion to the idea by arranging a mass marriage between his troops and Persian women. The "one world" idea has continued to exercise its influence over succeeding generations.

Above The east ceremonial staircase leading up to the Audience Hall, the Apadana, photographed from Xerxes' Throne Hall. At the center Median and Persian guards face an unfinished panel intended for an inscription. Medes wear round hats, Persians fluted hats. The figures behind march in the great New Year festival. The staircase, excavated only in 1932, is exceptionally well preserved.

Left An aerial view of the site, looking northeast, taken in the 1930s at an early stage of the excavations. It consists of a vast terrace built around a rocky headland at the foot of the mountains in the background. It was once surrounded by huge mud-brick walls. The various buildings can be identified from the plan on the following page.

Far left The head of a Persian prince wearing a battlemented crown, found at Persepolis. It is made of Egyptian blue frit and dates from the 5th or 4th centuries BC.

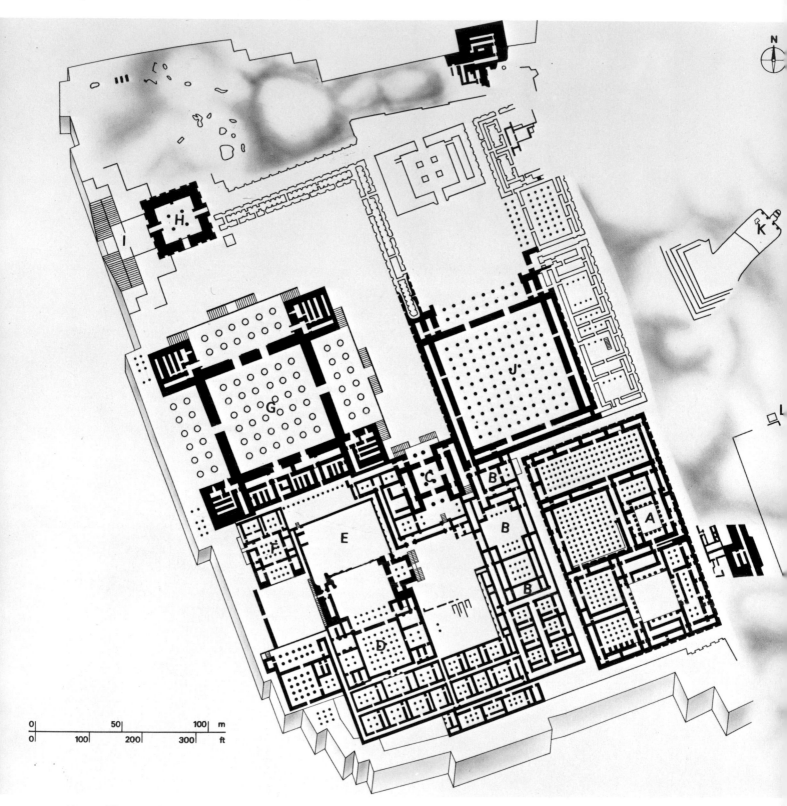

Above The ground plan of Persepolis gives some idea of the rather haphazard overall architectural scheme initiated by Darius I and brought to virtual completion by his son and grandson, Xerxes and Artaxerxes I. The careful positioning of Darius' great Audience Hall or Apadana **G**, with its monumental entrances, and the Throne Hall **J** behind with the Tripylon **C** linking the two is clear, but the rest seems to have been planned in a somewhat random manner, and indeed some of the building and final decoration remained unfinished. After his father Darius, Xerxes was the principal builder – that same Xerxes who tried and failed to humble Greece. He was responsible for the Gate House **H**, the beginning of the Throne Hall, his own palace **D** and for additions to the Treasury **A**, and he either rebuilt the Apadana with its east staircase, or added the staircase to Darius' building. The so-called Harem **B** was reconstructed to serve as an excavation house and is now a museum. **E** Ruined building. **F** Palace of Darius I. **I** Stairway to terrace. **K** Royal Tomb. **L** Cistern.

Top The Tripylon (Triple Gateway) at the southeast corner of Darius' great Audience Hall. The staircase is carved with figures of Median and Persian nobles and soldiers. The building, with easy access to any part of the platform, may have served as a central council house or banqueting hall.

Above An aerial view of the excavations in progress in the 1930s. Workmen are excavating the porch of the Throne Hall, and behind are the east staircase and the column bases and surviving columns of the huge Audience Hall of Darius I, with the palace of Darius to the left.

Above Among the beautifully carved stone reliefs decorating the east staircase of the Apadana is a series showing delegations from different parts of the Persian empire presenting gifts to the Great King. Each is escorted by a guard. On the top frieze are the Lydians leading a horse and diminutive chariot; below are the Bactrians leading a camel.

Right A procession of servants carrying dishes and young animals, probably for sacrifice, up the stairs of the palace of Darius.

Above A frieze in three registers on the east staircase depicting the king's horses in procession with Median and Persian nobles, identifiable as such by their headdresses and clothes. The Persians wear fluted hats and long flowing robes; the Medes wear rounded caps, trousers and short fitted coats, sometimes with a cloak.

Left Trees and tall-stemmed flowering plants form a highly stylized decoration on the east staircase of the Apadana.

KNOSSOS

The palace of King Minos on Crete

Until 1870, when the German archaeologist Heinrich Schliemann began to explore the ruins of Troy in northwest Asia Minor near the Hellespont, little was known about the brilliant Aegean civilization, the first in Europe, which flourished many centuries before Classical Greece. Homer's poems had sung of a golden age of heroes when Agamemnon, king of Mycenae, and his Greek warriors sacked Troy; while Thucydides and other Greek historians preserved a lingering tradition of a powerful King Minos of Knossos in Crete, whose naval power had dominated the Aegean long ago. Many of the Greek myths also seemed to reflect an earlier age of heroes, as in the famous story of Theseus and the Minotaur. At that time, it appeared, Athens itself was subject to the power of King Minos, who exacted an annual tribute of seven youths and seven maidens to feed to the Minotaur, a bull-headed monster who lived in the depths of a labyrinth. Theseus, the Athenian hero, slew the Minotaur and ran off with the king's daughter, Ariadne.

Schliemann's excavation actually confirmed the existence of ancient Troy and its sacking, and on the Greek mainland uncovered the Mycenae of Agamemnon, with its fabulous treasures. In Greece at least, Homer's fabled age of heroes was beginning to take on substance. But it was Arthur Evans, a wealthy English antiquarian, who was to establish the importance of the Bronze Age in Crete. Evans first saw the site of Knossos "brilliant with purple, white and pink anemones" on a March day in 1894. By 1900 he had bought the site and had started to excavate. The results were astounding, and Knossos became his life's work. Excavations showed that the enormous, many-chambered palace, a veritable labyrinth of a building, was surrounded by luxurious villas and was destroyed about 1400 BC. Obviously it was the wealthy capital of a sea empire, for it had no defensive walls. Built around a great central court, it had monumental staircases,

heavy pillars and a sophisticated drainage system. Its walls were decorated with lively frescoes, one at the north gate of a charging bull in relief, another of youths and maidens leaping over the back of a bull in a daring sport, still others showing ranks of spectators with elegantly dressed court ladies in front watching some such sport. Moreover, sealstones actually showed a Minotaur, with a bull's head and a man's body, probably of religious significance. The Theseus story began to make sense.

But more important, Evans and Schliemann, with their successors, had uncovered a brilliant new civilization, thus adding at least 2,000 years to the history of Greece. Of the two branches of this civilization, the Mycenaean (mainland) and the Minoan (Crete), Evans always believed the latter to be the dominant partner; but subsequent excavations have corrected this picture. For instance two types of inscribed clay tablets had been found in Crete, much alike except that the script on the older type (called Linear A) was obviously in a different language from that on the later type (called Linear B). Linear B tablets were at first found only at Knossos. Then in 1939 Carl Blegen found a hoard of Linear B tablets on the mainland, in the palace of Pylos, and the script also turned up at Mycenae and Thebes. By 1952 Michael Ventris, a brilliant young English architect, had succeeded in deciphering it. Linear B was Greek, though in a primitive form. Were Greeks from Mycenae, then, in control of Knossos in its last period? It had already been noted that the styles of art and the warlike aspect of the inhabitants of Knossos in its last phase were quite different from those associated with the earlier people of the palace's previous and greatest period. These earlier people were the short, lithe, spirited Minoans, of Mediterranean stock. The invaders, who wrote in Linear B, were the tall, bearded Mycenaeans, the Greek warriors of Homer's *Iliad*.

Yet their cultures were in most respects similar. Recent excavations in the whole Aegean area have helped to clarify the problem of chronology. Crete, it is now generally agreed, developed its civilization without a break from the Neolithic period (around 3500 BC) up to

Opposite "The Prince of the Lilies," one of the most famous of the frescoes found in the palace at Knossos. The original is now in the museum at Herakleion.

about 1500 BC. But shortly before the first great palaces were built in Crete (about 1930 BC) the developing civilization of the mainland suffered a check when invaders, probably the first Greeks, destroyed the main towns. Crete in the meantime reached its height after 1700 when Minoan fleets and Minoan culture dominated the Aegean. But about 1500 BC Cretan civilization was in turn disrupted, for a generation, by a catastrophic volcanic explosion on the island of Thera (see pp. 230–37) which did not, however, affect the mainland. Finally about 1450 BC the weakened Minoans fell prey to an invasion by mainland Greeks who had rapidly developed their culture under the strong influence of Crete. All the palaces were destroyed except Knossos, which the Greeks apparently used as their headquarters. Some 60 to 80 years later Knossos itself was destroyed in another invasion – perhaps from Mycenae itself, now overlord of the mainland. Thereafter Mycenae dominated the Aegean until about 1200 BC, when invasions, and internecine wars – of which the Trojan War was one – ushered in the Dark Ages.

Most of these phases, from the Neolithic onwards, are represented in the great site of Knossos. The palace, as partly reconstructed by Evans, stands on a man-made hill consisting of the debris of earlier settlements. Like all the Aegean palaces – Cretan or Mycenaean – Knossos served as an economic, administrative and ceremonial center for its surrounding territory, housing within it not only the king and royal court but the shrines, the artisans, the records and accounts, the storage rooms for olive oil, grains, wine, wool, cloth, pottery, weapons and chariots. These palaces were the focus of an entire civilization. Here indeed at Knossos was the awesome labyrinth of the Theseus legend. As Evans wrote: "The work of the spade has now brought out the essential and underlying truth of the old traditions that made Knossos the most ancient centre of civilized life in Greece and with it, of our whole continent."

Above right The "Snake Goddess," perhaps the most famous of all the objects found at Knossos. She is one of many terracotta statuettes of the Minoan household goddess found in Cretan shrines, and dates from around 1600–1550 BC. She was found in a small chest sunk into the floor of a shrine in the West Wing of the palace. The cat sitting on her head may be a royal symbol, but the meaning and ritual purpose of the figure as a whole are a mystery. Religion played an important part in Minoan life. It seems to have been an elaborate polytheism dominated by a female divinity. There were shrines on mountain tops and in palaces and mansions, as well as sacred caves. The main religious symbols were double axes mounted on poles and "horns of consecration" (stylized bull's horns – placed along the rooftop in the reconstruction opposite).

Opposite top Another scene from Knossos that has captured the world's imagination is the remarkable "bull-leaping" fresco from the East Wing of the palace. It depicts a boy (red) somersaulting over a bull's back, with two girls (always painted white) in attendance, and immediately calls to mind the legend of the Minotaur, the bull-headed monster to whom youths and maidens were sacrificed. The fresco is historical evidence of a perilous sport or ritual in which the performers risked their lives (and probably often lost them). The legend, the fresco, and other evidence such as the symbolic bull's "horns of consecration" found in the palace all attest the importance of the bull in Minoan religion and ritual.

Right A reconstruction of the West Wing of the palace, as envisaged by Sir Arthur Evans and drawn by his draftsman, Piet de Jong. Although only the foundations remained, terracotta plaques and models representing buildings, fresco paintings of columns and other pieces of evidence enabled the archaeologist to suggest the original appearance of the palace with some plausibility. The Throne Room lies inside to the right.

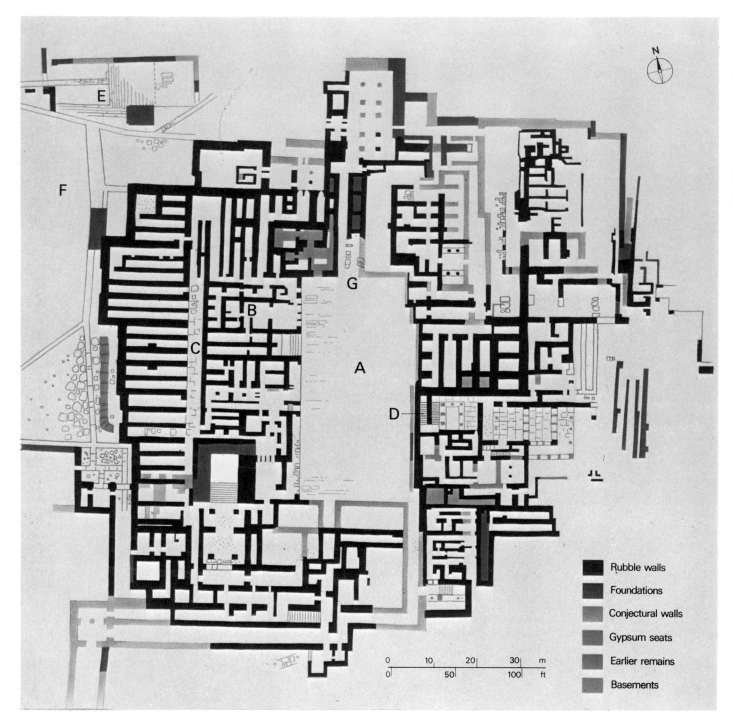

Rubble walls

Foundations

Conjectural walls

Gypsum seats

Earlier remains

Basements

0	10	20	30	m
0	50		100	ft

Above Ground plan of the palace site at Knossos. **A** Central Court. **B** Throne Room. **C** Western magazines, where the storage jars pictured opposite were found. **D** The Grand Staircase. **E** The Theatral Area, probably designed for the performance of religious rituals. **F** The West Court. **G** The Northern Entrance. The palace sits on a low hill near Herakleion consisting of the debris of centuries of building back into prehistory. The palace, and a system of stone-paved roads serving the town houses around it, was first laid out c. 1900 BC, was destroyed by earthquake c. 1700 BC, then rebuilt and modified. Final destruction came c. 1400 BC.

Top right A row of enormous storage jars, or *pithoi*, standing just as they were left when the palace was deserted. They would have been used to store oil, wine, grain and other products. The stone-built pits below them were probably used for the safekeeping of valuables.

Center right The northern entrance passage to the palace (G on the plan above), seen from the Central Court, looking north.

Right The top of the Grand Staircase (D), a masterpiece of sophisticated building, as reconstructed by Sir Arthur Evans. It consists of five flights of shallow stone steps around a central well, one or two rising above the central court, the rest below it, with landings leading off to spacious rooms and corridors.

Top The Throne Room (B, opposite), with the painted griffins guarding the throne patiently reconstructed from the fragments excavated. The Throne Room dates from the last, Mycenaean occupation of Knossos. Similar griffins guard the throne in the palace of Pylos on the Greek mainland.

Above The well-preserved road leading westward from the palace through the Minoan town nearby. Lined with fine houses and grandstands, it probably formed a route for processions. It meets the palace at the so-called Theatral Area (E on the plan opposite).

Above Two famous frescoes which once adorned the palace walls. The elegant woman (**left**) was probably a priestess in a religious cult scene, but she has been irretrievably nicknamed "la Parisienne." The Cupbearer (**right**) came from the southwestern part of the palace. Like most of the frescoes, it was found in fragmentary condition, but enough survived for the general outline of the figure to be restored. Both "la Parisienne" and the Cupbearer are now in the safety of the Herakleion museum.

Right A clay tablet inscribed with the script known as Linear B. Hundreds of such tablets were found at Knossos, and similar tablets were subsequently found on the Greek mainland. It was the English architect Michael Ventris who showed that the script on these tablets was an early form of Greek. The Knossos tablets date from around 1400 BC and earlier, the period when the Greek-speaking Mycenaeans from the mainland had conquered Crete. They are almost all inventory lists and are evidence of an elaborately centralized bureaucracy. The tablet illustrated here lists chariots and horses.

Left This fine Minoan vase, a *rhyton* or drinking cup in the shape of a bull's head, was exported to mainland Greece and was buried in a grave at Mycenae, dated around 1550–1500 BC. It shows the extent of Cretan influence when Knossos was at the height of its power.

Below An amphora (storage jar) found in the Old Palace, with decoration after the Cretan palm.

TUTANKHAMUN

Tomb treasures of an Egyptian pharaoh

In the history of archaeology there has never been anything quite like the sensation caused by the discovery of Tutankhamun's tomb in 1922. There have been innumerable books on the subject since then, as well as exhibitions, yet the appetite of the public for anything to do with "King Tut" still seems insatiable. There are good reasons for this: the story of the unknown "boy-king" who died at the threshold of manhood is an appealing one; the dazzling splendor and beauty of the treasures found in his small tomb, the only one in the Valley of the Kings ever to be found near-intact, was unprecedented, as was their remarkable state of preservation (what unimaginable treasures might have been found in the far larger tombs of the great pharaohs, all rifled and despoiled); and finally an important factor was the long-standing popularity of Egyptology ever since Napoleon invaded the country in 1798, taking along an army of artists and scholars to study and record the ancient monuments. The Valley of the Kings, the special burying place of the kings of the great 18th dynasty (1567–1342 BC) to which Tutankhamun belonged, had for long been a target for the native tomb robbers – as had the pyramids in far earlier centuries. In fact Tutankhamun's tomb had twice been entered shortly after his death, but with little damage, and had then been lost to sight. In the early 1900s a meticulous examination of the desolate Valley of the Kings was carried out by modern archaeologists, and one by one the sites of the rifled tombs of almost all the kings of the 18th dynasty were identified – except for that of Tutankhamun. Indeed an American archaeologist, Theodore Davis, who worked in the valley from 1903 to 1909, stumbled upon a cache of funerary equipment and other mementoes from Tutankhamun's tomb and decided that he had discovered the remains of the rifled tomb itself. He therefore wrote: "I

fear that the Valley of the Kings is now exhausted."

But an English Egyptologist, Howard Carter, thought otherwise. With the backing of Lord Carnarvon, a wealthy English aristocrat who had come to Egypt for his health, he began a systematic survey of a relatively unprobed sector of the Valley, feeling that Davis had misinterpreted certain small but significant clues as to the whereabouts of the young king's tomb. After years of fruitless work, and when he was almost ready to give up, in November 1922 Carter began to clear a last corner of his sector, covered by rubble and the remains of ancient workmen's huts. Below the huts a rock-cut step was revealed, then more steps. Sixteen steps down there was a plastered door with traces of seals, both of Tutankhamun and of the royal necropolis, showing that the tomb had been entered and resealed in antiquity. Behind this door a rubble-filled passage led to a second door. Knocking a hole in this door Carter, and then Carnarvon, peered through and saw for the first time the jumbled treasures within – large animal-shaped beds, alabaster vases, chests, flowers, gilded chariot wheels, a magnificent throne – all glittering with gold and bright colors. Carter was overwhelmed by "the gorgeousness of the sight." Tutankhamun's tomb had been discovered; the news was flashed to the world.

It took Carter two years just to repair and preserve on the spot, and then remove, this vast accumulation in the antechamber. Then came the burial chamber with the four gilded shrines and within them the three nested coffins, one of solid gold, and the mummy itself with a magnificent gold mask covering its face, and finally the treasures in the annex and the so-called treasury. The work within the tomb was completed by 1928, the last report on the excavation published in 1933. Carter, helped by a team of experts and by the American photographer, Harry Burton, had done an outstanding job, one which marked the coming of age of scientific archaeology.

Tutankhamun was an extremely minor king whose brief reign of just some ten years came during the 14th century BC, near the end of the 18th dynasty. He was the son-in-law, and possibly a son or half-brother, of

Opposite The famous gold death mask of Tutankhamun, surely a close portrait of the dead king. "The youthful Pharaoh was before us at last . . . Here was the climax of our long researches!" wrote Howard Carter, the archaeologist who excavated the almost untouched tomb of the king, recalling the moment of discovery in 1925. The solid gold is inlaid with semiprecious stones and glass paste.

Akhenaten the heretic king who had created a new capital at Akhetaten (Tell el-Amarna) and devoted himself to the worship of one god, the Aten. After Akhenaten's death a reaction set in, and when the young Tutankhamun came to the throne his advisers, Ay, a relative, and Horemheb, the army commander (powers behind the throne), took the occasion to complete the overthrow of Akhenaten's revolution, return the court to the old capital of Thebes and restore the old state religion of Amun. Tutankhamun, however, had been brought up during Akhenaten's great revolution, which as well as being political and religious had markedly liberalized the traditional arts of Egypt; and this goes far to explain the exceptional grace and realism of the art found in the young king's tomb.

On coming to the throne Tutankhamun had been married to Ankhesenamun, the young widow (and third daughter) of Akhenaten. When Tutankhamun died young his queen, whose next husband would inherit the throne, was at the mercy of the two non-royal "advisers," Ay and Horemheb. Terrified but determined to safeguard the dynasty, she took the unprecedented step of writing (as we know from the Hittite archives) to the king of the Hittites, who ruled in what is now Turkey: "My husband is dead and I have no son ... If you send me one of your sons he will become my husband for it is repugnant to me to take one of my servants to husband." The Hittite king could not believe it: mighty Egypt asking his son to become pharaoh! But Ankhesenamun wrote again: "You do not believe me ... I have written only to you ... Give me one of your sons and he will be my husband and lord of the land of Egypt." So the Hittite king dispatched a prince. But someone (perhaps Horemheb or Ay) had him murdered on the way. Ay finally married Ankhesenamun, and he ruled four years, to be succeeded by Horemheb. Unleashing a reign of terror, Horemheb made every effort to wipe out all traces of the hated Amarna family, including Tutankhamun, and he razed Akhenaten's capital at Tell el-Amarna to the ground. Thus ended the 18th dynasty. But thanks to Carter and Carnarvon, Tutankhamun has gloriously survived.

Tutankhamun's tomb lay concealed close to that of Ramesses VI. Both lay under the "Peak" (**above left**), whose pyramid shape may have been one of the reasons why the New Kingdom rulers selected this valley as a burial site. Carter's first glimpse of the tomb interior revealed the jumbled treasures in the antechamber (**above**); thieves had penetrated this far but got away with very little. The gilded chariot wheels, the ornamented chests, the beds in the shape of animals were but a foretaste of the wonders that were to be revealed. Carter and his men first had to clear the antechamber and then break through the sealed door into the burial chamber, which was all but filled with an immense shrine of gilded wood. Within it two more gilded shrines, one within the other, were opened and finally a fourth (**far left**), which revealed a magnificent red sandstone sarcophagus. The following pages show the opening of the three coffins within the sarcophagus. A first view of the treasury (**left**), subsequently opened up beyond the burial chamber, shows a gilded chest with carrying poles, and on it a statue of the god Anubis, wrapped in linen. At the back is the canopic shrine, with one of its guardian goddesses visible, which held the mummified viscera of the king.

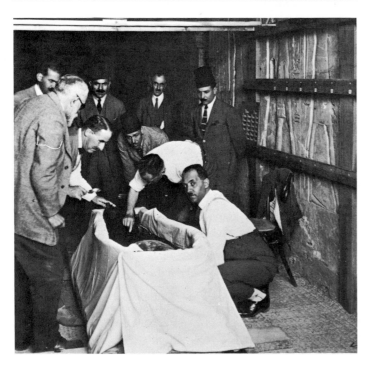

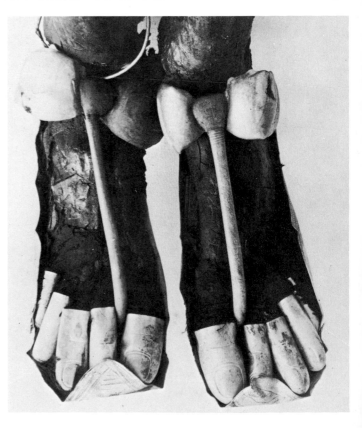

The sandstone sarcophagus was opened to reveal the first of three mummiform coffins, nested one within the other. In Burton's photograph (**opposite, top left**) Carter, careful archaeologist that he was, dusts the nose of the face on the second coffin. When this was lifted (**opposite, center left**) tackle had to be used.

The features of the second coffin (**above left**) were painted to represent the suffering of death. Those of the third and innnermost coffin (**above center** and **opposite, top right**) showed great serenity, symbolizing the

fortitude of the pharaoh as he awaited his resurrection from death. Elaborate ritual and symbolism governed the choice of equipment, the decoration and even the layout in a pharaoh's tomb. When first revealed, the inner coffin was wrapped in a red linen shroud folded back to show the face alone. A necklace of flowers lay across the breast. The purpose of the funeral ritual and its intricate symbolism was to bring the dead king safely into the afterlife with his body intact and all his worldly possessions about him.

The two outer coffins were of gilded wood,

but the third was made of solid 22-carat gold. Inside, the mummy itself was finally discovered, swathed in wrappings. When these were removed (**opposite, bottom left**) the famous gold death mask (see p. 126), a masterpiece of portraiture, was found on the head. Unfortunately the mummy of the king (**above right,** with the death mask in place) turned out to be badly damaged by over-lavish use of unguents. However, the feet (**left**), partially encased in golden sheaths and sandals, and the hands were well preserved.

Above Among the treasures discovered in the tomb was this ornate fan, placed with other objects between the second and third gilded shrines. It originally held ostrich feathers. On one side (top) the king is seen with his dogs and his bow and arrow, hunting an ostrich, and on the other side he is returning in triumph, with bearers carrying the game before him.

Left The third and innermost coffin, of pure gold. It weighs almost 2,500 lb. The incised design shows the interlaced wings of the protective goddesses Isis and Nephthys, and on the king's arms the wings of the great goddesses of Upper and Lower Egypt, a vulture and a serpent. Inside was the mummy of Tutankhamun, among whose wrappings were close to 150 pieces of gold jewelry.

Opposite On the side of a small chest was found this gold relief portraying Tutankhamun and his young wife Ankhesenamun. The elegance and informality of the work reflect the revolution in style brought about by Akhenaten, Tutankhamun's heretic predecessor.

Left A vulture pendant, just one example of the hundreds of pieces of jewelry found throughout the tomb – pendants, pectorals, rings, earrings – some almost over-ornate in their complexity. Materials used included gold, lapis-lazuli, cornelian, turquoise, feldspar, alabaster, chalcedony and glazed terracotta.

Right A royal dagger with decorated sheath and pommel. If this makeshift tomb was so rich in treasures, those of the far greater pharaohs must have been splendid beyond belief, with many more chambers and even more splendid objects. It took ten years (1922–1932) to clear this one small tomb of its treasures.

Below right An alabaster lamp representing the stems, leaves and flowers of the lotus plant. The central flower is fully open while those on the sides are still in bud. They rise from stems with a horizontal leaf spreading out sidewise. Alabaster, with its milky beauty, was the material used for unguent jars, vases, cups, chests and many other objects in the tomb.

Below left Another touchingly natural and affectionate scene representing Tutankhamun and his wife. It formed part of the backrest of the gold-plated throne found in the antechamber. The young king is seated quite informally on his throne (the informality of the pose is again a legacy from the liberating years of Tutankhamun's predecessor, Akhenaten), while the queen leans forward gracefully. She appears to be anointing the king's elaborate collar in a gesture of affection. She wears a similar collar. Sheets of gold and silver, with inlays of colored glass paste, calcite and glazed ceramic were used to create this splendid scene. It is clear that the burial of Tutankhamun, a very minor pharaoh who was only 19 when he died, was hastily arranged and the grave goods assembled in a most haphazard manner. Yet his tomb in the Valley of the Kings is the only one to have survived virtually intact, and the splendor of his funeral goods are now the astonishment of the world.

Far right The three-foot-high solid gold statue of the goddess Selket, one of four miniature goddesses standing guard over the gilded wooden shrine which contained the mummified viscera of the king.

THE PERSIAN REVIVAL

Rock reliefs of the Sasanian kings

Not far from Persepolis, the famous palace of the Achaemenid kings of ancient Persia (see p. 111 above), lies Naqsh-i Rustam where the native guides, with a good deal of pride, will show the tourist the cruciform tombs of the kings Darius and Xerxes cut into the face of a cliff in the fifth century BC. But with even more pride they will point out the bold reliefs of the Sasanian kings of Persia, cut into the same cliff many centuries later as if to identify themselves with the glory of the ancient Achaemenids. They will single out especially one that shows the Roman emperor kneeling in supplication before his captor, the great warrior Shapur I. Shapur, an imposing figure of a man, is seated on his heavy charger with one hand resting on his sword, the very image of a conqueror.

The Sasanians, and their predecessors the Parthians, though a source of pride to the modern Persian, are to the West the forgotten people of Middle Eastern history. We remember the Persia of Cyrus, Darius and Xerxes because of the Greek wars, the Bible (Cyrus released the Jews from their Babylonian captivity) and Alexander the Great, who destroyed the Persian empire, Yet for nearly 800 years, between the fall of Alexander's successors, the Seleucids, and the onslaught of the Arabs in the 7th century AD, the Parthians and then the Sasanians, thriving on the east–west trade between Rome and the Orient, ruled a Persian empire which at times equaled that of the Achaemenids, reaching east to India, south to southern Arabia and west, briefly, to Syria and Egypt. The Sasanians in particular carried on the Aryan traditions and the Zoroastrian religion of the ancient Achaemenids. Both people, though little known to us, impinged on the history of the West in a number of ways. Above all they were the scourge and rival of Rome on its eastern borders throughout most of its

history, from the Battle of Carrhae in 53 BC when the wily Crassus, member of the First Triumvirate with Caesar and Pompey, lost his life and his army to the Parthians, up to the Byzantine emperor Heraclius who nearly defeated the Sasanians in the 7th century AD, just before their empire fell to the Arabs. Such well-known Romans as Mark Antony and the emperors Tiberius, Nero, Trajan, Marcus Aurelius, Septimius Severus and Caracalla mounted Parthian campaigns with varying success. The Emperor Gordian and later Julian the Apostate died fighting the Sasanians. Valerian died in captivity, while the hordes of Roman prisoners captured in such campaigns, many of them skilled engineers or artisans, were put to work building bridges and palaces, or carving the rock reliefs for the Sasanian kings.

The early Sasanian kings were vigorous, despotic rulers of a semi-feudal nation, often at war but also great builders of palaces and cities. The dynasty was founded by Ardashir, a dynamic, hawk-nosed, full-bearded man who about 209 AD became king of Pars or Persis, the heartland province of the Persians in which Persepolis is situated. His overlords the Parthians, originally nomads from the east who had ruled in Persia since the 3rd and 2nd centuries BC, had by now been dangerously weakened by disastrous wars against Rome, by plague, and by economic troubles. Ardashir soon became virtually independent, building himself a magnificent palace and a fortress at Firuzabad and laying out there a great circular city defended by strong walls. The Parthian king, offended, wrote him: "You miserable Kurd, how dare you build such a royal residence?" But Ardashir ignored this apparent insult. In 224 AD he felt strong enough to challenge the king, with the aid of some Mesopotamian allies. In the ensuing battle Artabanus V was killed and Ardashir, now King of Kings himself, consciously set out to recreate the old Achaemenid empire, setting up a strong central government, reforming the coinage and establishing Zoroastrianism as the state religion. His descendants were to rule for 400 years. His son, Shapur I, was to prove as able a ruler as his father. He too established

Opposite The first Sasanian rock reliefs were carved by the founder of the dynasty, Ardashir, near his newly-established fortress (now Firuzabad). In the scene above, part of a 60-foot frieze, Ardashir himself is portrayed unhorsing his Parthian opponent, Artabanus V. On the gold coin below, Ardashir is shown wearing the jeweled crown of his great Parthian predecessor Mithridates.

a city, his favorite capital of Bishapur.

Ardashir's rule, as well as his art and architecture, bore a distinctively Sasanian stamp from the beginning. In his building he introduced the dome and the *iwan*, a great arched entranceway, both thereafter elements in Islamic Persian architecture up to the present, and in his rock reliefs (perhaps with an eye on the sculptures of Persepolis) he created a new "official" art to proclaim the supremacy of the Sasanian kings. Ardashir celebrated his defeat of Artabanus; his son Shapur his triumphs over Rome whom he considered to be his only worthy rival. In a battle in 244 AD Shapur brought about the death of the Roman Emperor Gordian III, whose successor, Philip the Arab, had to sue for peace and pay a stiff ransom; in 256 he destroyed a Roman army of 60,000 men, and in 260 (in his own words) "Valerian Caesar himself with our own hand we made captive. And the rest, the Pretorian Prefect, senators and generals, and whatever of that force were officers, all we made captive and away to Persis we led (them)." For the next 150 years nearly every Sasanian king carved a rock relief, after which the tradition lapsed. The Sasanian rock relief appeared for the last time in the 7th century, during the final great period of Sasanian history when Khusrau II, a flamboyant conqueror, remembered in later Persian poetry for his romance with Shirin, his Christian concubine, built Taq-i Bustan, a huge *iwan* carved out of the solid rock and decorated with superb reliefs of hunting scenes. At its back, along with the usual investiture scene, he had carved a magnificent relief of himself in full knightly armor astride his famous horse, Shabdiz. Only a few decades later the Sasanians disappeared forever with the triumph of the armies of Islam.

The general outline of the jousting scenes on the Firuzabad relief can be seen clearly in the sketch by the French artist Eugène Flandin (**below**), while details are picked out in the photographs. The principal figure is Ardashir (**far right**), toppling the horse of the Parthian king Artabanus V. Ardashir's hair, gathered into a bunch above his head to form the Sasanian royal *korymbos*, has lost its silken covering and is shown streaming out behind. In the center is Ardashir's son Shapur, unseating the Parthian Grand Vizier Darbendan. The impact of the Sasanian lances has caused the Parthians and their horses to fall. Shapur's animal-headed cap is the insignia of the crown prince. In addition to their headgear, the Sasanians can be identified by the crests shown on their horses' caparisons. This can clearly be seen (**right** and **below**) where a Sasanian knight, grasping his opponent around the neck, has swept him from his horse.

Top One great theme of the Sasanian rock reliefs was the triumph of the king over his enemies. The other was the investiture of the king by his favorite god, usually Ahuramazda, the senior god of the Zoroastrian religion which the Sasanians practiced. For his investiture scene Ardashir I (ruled 224–242 AD) chose the cliffs of Naqsh-i Rustam near Persepolis, where the tomb of the Persian king Darius I had been carved many centuries earlier. In the investiture above Ahuramazda is handing the king a diadem. Beneath the god's feet (detail **above**) the spirit of evil, Ahriman, is being trampled, while beneath Ardashir's horse is the corpse of the defeated Parthian king.

Right The investiture of Bahram I (ruled 273–276 AD), cut into a cliff face at Bishapur, 50 miles west of Persepolis. Ahuramazda, on

the left, is handing the king his diadem. The horses' legs have been cut off by a later water channel, and the corpse below the king was added later; it may represent Bahram's grandson who was deposed by Narseh (ruled 293–302 AD).

Above The investiture of Shapur I (ruled 243–273 AD) by Ahuramazda. This relief is carved in the walls of a small grotto at Naqsh-i Rajab near Persepolis.

Left The investiture of Ardashir II, a later king who ruled 379–383 AD. This relief is at Taq-i Bustan, about 150 miles northwest of Isfahan. The king is on the left receiving his diadem from Ahuramazda, and behind the king is the god Mithra, standing on a lotus, his halo representing the rays of the sun. After this period the custom of cutting royal reliefs lapsed until the 7th century, just before the destruction of the Sasanian empire.

Above To celebrate his triumphs over the Romans, Shapur I had two huge reliefs carved on either side of the gorge at Bishapur. The two reliefs are closely similar in subject and composition, and each consists of a central panel surrounded by additional registers, depicting Sasanian cavalry and tributaries. The relief on the left bank is shown above. In the central panel shown in close-up (**left**) Shapur is sitting on his horse holding the captive emperor Valerian by the hand. Under his horse's feet is the corpse of the emperor Gordian, and before him is the kneeling figure of Philip the Arab, his successor, who was forced to sue for peace.

The relief on the right bank is smaller and in a different style, and may have been executed by foreign (perhaps captive Roman) craftsmen. The central panel (**top right**) has the same subjects as the left bank. Also illustrated here are details from the supporting registers: Sasanian cavalry (**center right**), Valerian's captured chariot (**right**) and a group of tributaries (**above**).

The final flowering of Sasanian rock relief art came early in the 7th century under Khusrau II (ruled 591–628), whose grandfather, Khusrau I (ruled 531–579) had revived the Sasanian empire after a period of decline. At Taq-i Bustan Khusrau II, a mighty warrior, had a magnificent archway (an *iwan*) cut into the solid rock. At the rear of the arch was carved a splendid equestrian statue of the king on his favorite charger, Shabdiz (**above**), his spear poised for action, with a helmet covering his whole face and leaving only slits for the eyes – a knight in armor many centuries before the European Middle Ages. The side walls were decorated with hunting scenes in relief, details of which are shown here: a deer-hunt (**right**) and a boar-hunt (**opposite**).

THE FORBIDDEN CITY

The imperial palace at Peking

The Forbidden City, now a museum, is the only surviving example of an imperial palace in China. The rectangular palace area is walled and moated; its residential quarters were closed to all but the emperor, the empress and her sons, the imperial concubines, the women attendants and eunuch servants. The Forbidden City is enclosed within another rectangle, the Imperial City, which in turn lies within Peking's North City, also called the Tartar or the Inner City. This, with the Outer (or Chinese) City to the south, made up the original walled capital of Peking. The palace as it now stands was built in the early Ming period, between 1405 and 1420, a comparatively late date in the long perspective of Chinese history. But in many ways the palace today touches on and illuminates many basic aspects of the entire history of China.

Chinese history differs markedly from that of the West. Although the civilization of the West actually has far older roots, that of China *seems* much older because of its remarkable continuity over some 3,000 years, from the Bronze Age Shang kings of about 1500 BC to the near present. Like the West in Roman times, China suffered many barbarian invasions from the north, including the Mongols under Kublai Khan and his successors, the later Manchus and many lesser incursions. But there were no Dark Ages after these onslaughts, for the invaders were few and the Chinese many, and such was the strength of Chinese culture that it would invariably absorb its invaders or drive them out. Perhaps this was because China was a whole civilization rather than a European-style nation-state, and was stabilized from early times by the family clan with its inner cohesion and its respect for tradition and for the ways and memory of the ancestors. From early times the Chinese kept careful histories. Unlike

the West, they had no need to rediscover their classical heritage, for they never lost it. Archaeology has strikingly confirmed this continuity of culture. The first crude Chinese script, scratched on the Shang oracle bones of about 1100 BC, can still be read by scholars today; and a list of early Shang kings on these bones is closely paralleled by a similar list in a 1st-century BC history. Yet these bones were only recently excavated! China came quickly to maturity after the first unification of the country in the 3rd century BC and was ruled from then until 1912 by an emperor (there never was any other political system) – a father figure in his palace, served by a bureaucracy of scholar-gentlemen, at first appointed and later chosen by examination, who owed loyalty only to the emperor. The old aristocracy was very early subordinated to this class. But even the emperor, considered as the father of his people as well as the "Son of Heaven," could be deposed if it was thought that he had "exhausted the mandate of Heaven." Only the civilization itself of China, which had developed in geographical isolation, seemed unshakable and immortal. It only began to be broken down by the brutal intrusion of the West in the 19th century.

In many ways the palace at Peking exemplifies the continuity of Chinese culture. It has seen much history. Here on February 12, 1912, over 2,000 years after Shih Huang Ti, the "First Emperor," had united the country, the last of the Manchu emperors was forced to abdicate in favor of a republic. From this palace too, the cruel and reactionary Empress Dowager Tzu Hsi, surrounded by her women and her eunuchs, presided for nearly 50 years over the gradual dissolution of China until she died in 1908. Here in 1644, on a hill in the palace grounds, the last Ming emperor hanged himself, opening the way for the founding of the foreign Manchu dynasty. And nearly 240 years earlier the Forbidden City itself had been built by Yung Lo, the third Ming emperor, who had moved his capital from Nanking to Peking, former capital of the Mongols, whom the Mings had driven out. He rebuilt the city along the spacious lines laid out by the Mongol Kublai Khan and, possibly, built his palace, the Forbidden City,

Opposite above Looking across the courtyard to T'ai Ho Tien, the Hall of Supreme Harmony, the throne hall and audience chamber. This graceful building is the focal point of the palace, and was regarded as the center of the universe.

Below The Emperor's throne room in the Hall of Supreme Harmony, now a museum.

on the site of Kublai's own palace, which had so dazzled Marco Polo. But the Forbidden City, which took only 15 years to complete with the labor of a million men, had far earlier antecedents, as had the plan of Peking itself.

Chinese buildings, even the most magnificent, consisted basically of wooden pillars supporting a tiled roof, hence few ancient buildings have survived. The most important structures, however, were often rebuilt, but always on the same plan, so that a palace like the Forbidden City reflects styles that have changed little since the early centuries of Chinese civilization. Moreover, from very early times the Chinese laid out their cities, their palaces, their shrines, even their gardens in rectilinear patterns, always aligned north to south, the latter being the favored direction of holiness. The patterns and the alignment reflected the divine plan of the orderly, balanced universe. All this is seen in Peking and its Forbidden City. And it was seen, too, in Peking's most illustrious predecessor, the great city of Ch'angan, of which little now remains. Ch'angan was a capital of the Han Dynasty (206 BC–220 AD) which carved

Above A panoramic view of the Forbidden City, looking from the northwest. The tallest roof in the center of the picture is that of the Hall of Supreme Harmony. All the roofs are of yellow glazed tiles, yellow being the imperial color reserved for the emperor.

out the first great Chinese empire, subduing much of central Asia and discovering the Roman West. Later, as the capital of the even more brilliant T'ang empire (618–906 AD), it contained nearly two million people. Walled and covering about 30 square miles, it was laid out in a grid pattern with the "Great Luminous Palace" at the northern end. The city was destroyed by a warlord in 906 AD, but a plan of the palace dating from the 7th century survives, and the similarity to Peking is striking. Thus the Forbidden City, built in the 15th century, faithfully reflects an architectural tradition established many centuries earlier.

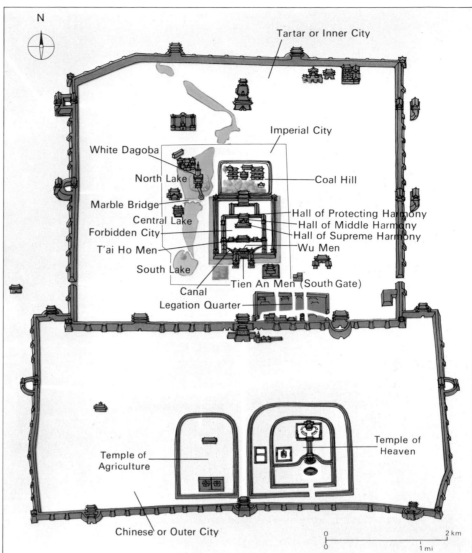

Above right A sketch map showing the ground plan of the walled city of Peking as it was in 1949, with its Outer City, Inner City, Imperial City and finally the moated Forbidden City. It was then little changed since Ming times.

Right The ground plan of the ancient Chinese capital of Ch'angan as it was in the 7th century AD, showing the traditional pattern followed in Peking. Ch'angan was destroyed in 906 AD. Only the Great Swallow (Ta Yen) pagoda now remains. The Ta Ming Kung or Great Brilliant Palace was built in 634 AD. The imperial palace was an earlier construction.

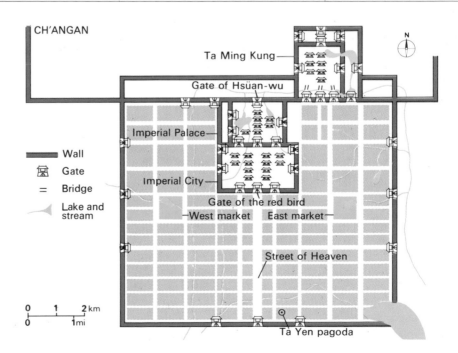

Top The Ti'en An Men, Gate of Heavenly Peace, the southern outer gate of the Forbidden City (see plan on previous page).

Above The first courtyard of the Forbidden City, between the Wu Men (Military Gate) and the T'ai Ho Men (Gate of Great Harmony), looking north. The court is crossed by a sinuous canal with five bridges.

Above A marble slab with a dragon carved in relief. The marble came from Yünnan, some 2,000 miles away. This and other such slabs were set between the tiers of steps leading up to the throne halls.

Above The Wu Men, or Military Gate of the Forbidden City, headquarters of the Imperial Guard. This picture is taken from the inner courtyard, looking southwards. The soldiers' barracks were in a courtyard between the two south gates, and no soldiers were allowed any further into the Forbidden City.

Right The Chung Ho Tien, Hall of Middle Harmony, and the Pao Ho Tien, Hall of Protecting Harmony, lesser imperial audience halls, both set in line on a terrace behind the Hall of Supreme Harmony. The steps and carved balustrades are made of white marble.

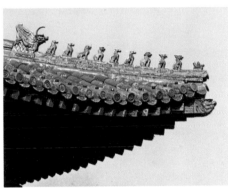

Above These stylized figures sitting on a roof cornice represent guardian spirits to ward off evil. Evil spirits were thought to gain entrance to houses through their cornices. The figures are typical of the intricately-carved detail to be found throughout the Forbidden City.

Opposite This magnificent door leads into the residential part of the palace. The door itself is richly carved and the door surround is decorated with tiles. The residential quarters, where the women and children of the imperial family lived, were strictly guarded by eunuchs, and no males were allowed to enter (with the possible exception of doctors).

Top These huge gilt bronze bowls stand in the courtyard before the Hall of Supreme Harmony. They were used as water tanks in case of fire, for the walls of the audience halls are made of wood and were always a severe fire hazard. Note the elaborate decoration on the bastion of the wall behind.

Above A house with lattice windows along its south wall in the private residential part of the palace. Such rooms were used mainly in the hot summer, when the lattices would allow air to circulate but exclude direct sunlight.

Above View over the palace roofs towards Coal Hill, an artificial mound made, not of coal, but of earth excavated from the palace moat. In a pavilion on the hill the last Ming emperor took his life in 1644. The building now on the hill is the White Dagoba, a shrine of later date.

Right A gigantic bronze incense burner standing in the palace gardens. The northern, residential part of the palace consisted of small courtyards with lanes and gardens, much like a small Chinese city.

Opposite A temple in the palace gardens, probably merely for ornament as no Buddhists would be allowed in the palace, the home of the Confucian emperor.

PART FOUR

The Living and the Dead

FROM CRADLE TO GRAVE

Daily life of ancient Greece

The dazzling achievements of the ancient Greeks in art, architecture, literature and philosophy sometimes make it difficult for us to accept that the creators of all this beauty of hand and mind were not demigods but people. Even the greatest of them, a Pericles or a Plato, went through the petty traumas of childhood and schooling and had to submit to the authority of their parents. They fell in love, were married; they took up an occupation, enjoyed feasts, got outrageously drunk; they had their share of troubles, both personal and national; they grew old, died and were buried. As figures in history, too, the Greeks are often thought of as beyond reproach. There is for instance the famous image of a handful of brave warriors standing up to the barbarous hordes of the Persians and defeating them. This of course was true, but if we look more closely into Greek history we find that a substantial number of Greeks were actually fighting on the Persian side, that Xenophon led his famous 10,000 into Asia on behalf of a Persian pretender, and that in the 4th century some 50,000 Greeks – a large number for a relatively small country – were fighting abroad as mercenaries for whoever would pay them the most. Then there was the endless petty squabbling of the city-states, which makes it all the more remarkable that most of them were able to unite to defeat the Persians. There is detectable, too, an unpleasant note of arrogance, especially in Athens, reputedly noblest of all the cities. Her attack against the rich Sicilian city of Syracuse in 415 BC, for instance, seems to have been an act of sheer aggression, as we would put it. There is also the fact that the Greek city-states held huge slave populations. It has been estimated that in the 5th century BC there were 60,000 to 80,000 slaves in Athens alone, compared to perhaps some 40,000 to 45,000 male adult citizens. Women in a citizen's family had no more legal or political rights than slaves. Love between men, or between men and boys, was for many the noblest form of love.

One could go on, but the object is not to expose the feet of clay on the Greek statue but to emphasize the fact that the Greeks, brilliant as they were, were human. Nothing brings this out more clearly than a study of the daily life of the Greeks, of the poor and humble as well as the rich and famous. The sources are abundant, the most important being Greek literature, which is most informative about Athens in the 5th and 4th centuries BC. This is supplemented by the material remains, both objects of daily use and pictures of everyday scenes, such as are presented on the following pages. The setting for this daily life was the *polis*, the city-state, which included the countryside as well as the city. The leading Greek city-states were very small, perhaps numbering 50,000 people on average, with Athens at its height reaching only about 275,000, including men, women, children, aliens and slaves. Even for the privileged, daily life was simple and austere. The houses were unpretentious, inward-looking, with usually a separate quarter for the women at the back where they spent much of their lives. The men used the house only for eating, sleeping and the occasional banquet, spending most of their time out of doors in the golden sunlight of Greece. Unless they were unwanted and exposed to die, children grew up with the mother until the age of seven, when the boys would generally be sent to school, accompanied by a slave or pedagogue, until their eighteenth year. Their education comprised letters (reading, writing, and learning poetry by heart) music, some arithmetic and much athletics and gymnastics. The girls stayed at home, learning domestic chores from their mother and perhaps some reading and writing, until the age of about 15, when they were given away in marriage. After a joyous wedding they were carried off by their husbands who thereafter reimposed the strict control formerly exercised by their father.

It was a man's world, and the Greek male was a

Opposite above Greek commercial life. This cup, dated about 560 BC, depicts King Arkesilas of Cyrene (a colony in North Africa) supervising the weighing and storing of sacks of some unknown commodity.

Below A Greek religious ceremony on a painted wooden votive plaque from near 6th-century BC Corinth. The procession, which includes two musicians, is leading an animal to be sacrificed at the altar on the right.

gregarious creature, spending much of his time in the agora or marketplace, or in the barber shop in conversation, or at the gymnasium or stadium taking part in sports or military training, for every male citizen was liable for military service from 18 to 60. Citizens were also obliged to spend time on the ruling council, or as magistrates, or attending the popular assembly. Some owned factories, making pottery or shields, while others engaged in commerce, exporting vases, olives or wine. But the staple occupation was, as always, agriculture, and many town-dwelling citizens also owned farms in the country. In the evening the Greek might relax at one of the numerous dinner parties, all-male affairs which were often followed by a "symposium," an evening of drinking, talk and entertainment, with dancing girls and musicians, acrobats and games. There could be good talk, or an orgy might develop. But the most important entertainments, open to all, even to women, were the many poetry recitals,

singing and dancing displays, sports and dramatic performances which formed part of the religious festivals – for the Greek gods were pleased by the same things that humans liked: food, drink, flowers, works of art, dancing, music and sports. The festivals were great civic and national occasions and inspired many of the Greeks' finest achievements, the drama for instance arising out of Athens' Greater Dionysia, the festival of the god Dionysus. So the Greeks were kept busy all their lives, and when an important Greek came to die there was yet another ceremony, a magnificent funeral with professional mourners, a procession and a great funeral pyre, after which the ashes were laid to rest under one of those lovely monuments showing the deceased as if in the joyful prime of life. An inscription on one Athenian monument reads: "After many pleasant sports with my companions, I who sprang from earth am earth once more."

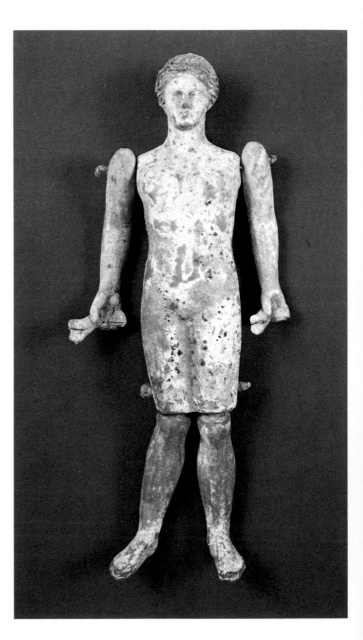

Top A child in a "potty-chair," painted on a Greek vase. An actual example of such a potty-chair was found in the excavations of the Agora (civic center) of Athens.

Above A baby's bottle made of black-painted terracotta, the equivalent of glass in ancient Athens.

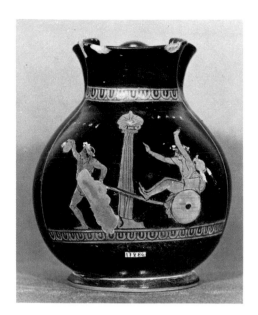

Top Two young boys playing with a "go-cart." They are depicted on one of the small jugs given to children in Athens at the time of the annual spring festival.

Above Youths playing a game that resembles modern hockey, part of a relief carved on an Athenian marble funerary monument of the late 6th century BC.

Top right A Greek school, redrawn from a vase. On the left is a lesson on the lyre, on the right a pupil reads some verses written on a slate. A pedagogue, or slave attendant, sits and waits at the right.

Center right Singing to the accompaniment of an *aulos* (not a flute but a pipe or double-pipe), next in popularity to the lyre. Music was an important part of Greek education, and most poetry was sung or recited to musical accompaniment.

Right Greek school exercises, written in ink on a wooden tablet, from Egypt in the Ptolemaic (Greek) period. Schoolchildren might also use wax tablets, incised with a pointed stylus.

Left A child's terracotta doll, with hinged arms. It was no doubt dressed by its owner.

Left Women fetching and carrying water from a public fountain, painted on an Athenian black-figure vase, about 525 BC. Greek households did not have piped water, but depended on communal wells, cisterns and fountains. Fetching water was therefore an important domestic duty as well as a social occasion. It was always carried out by women, as were all domestic tasks.

Below Young women washing at a basin, depicted on a red-figure vase. The woman on the left has taken off her fashionable boots, and appears to be holding a towel. The one in the center is holding a scent jar in her right hand, and is washing herself with what looks like a sponge on a stick.

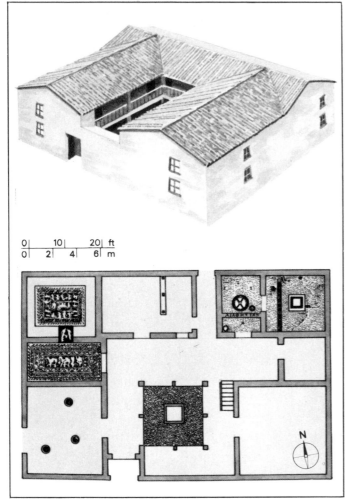

Above A plan and artist's impression of a Greek house, based on excavations. The rooms are typically arranged around a south-facing colonnaded courtyard with an altar near its center. The chief room is the *andron* or men's reception room, indicated here in the northwest corner. Both the *andron* and an adjoining room have elaborate pebble mosaics on their floors.

Above A terracotta model of bakers kneading dough for bread. The scale of operations indicated suggests that baking bread could be a large-scale specialized commercial enterprise, rather like a modern bakery.

Right This charming terracotta figurine, dating from the 5th century BC, shows an Athenian woman grinding corn.

Above A men's drinking party or symposium, depicted on a red-figure cup (early 5th century BC). Plato's *Symposium* describes an evening of high-minded conversation, but the symposium was more likely to be an occasion for drunken debauchery, with entertainment provided by naked flute girls, acrobats and dancers.

Left Warfare was a constant feature of Greek life, and all male citizens had to serve in the army (or, for the lower classes, row in the galleys). This detail of a frieze on the Vix krater, a large bronze vessel of the 6th century BC, shows a Greek hoplite (footsoldier) with his shield and plumed helmet, followed by the horses of a chariot. The hoplite was the mainstay of the Greek army.

Opposite Boxing and wrestling, depicted on an Athenian vase of about 525 BC. The Greeks were intensely competitive and devoted much of their time to the gymnasium and to sports of all kinds including athletics, boxing, wrestling and chariot racing. Between the two boxers is the potter's signature, "Nikosthenes made me."

Above A wedding procession winds around a vase. The bride and groom, holding hands, are led to their house by friends and relatives, accompanied by a flute-girl and torch-bearers. This was the central feature of the wedding.

Below Dancing girls, probably taking part in a religious festival. They come from a frieze on the gateway of the sanctuary of the Great Gods on the northeast Aegean island of Samothrace (4th century BC).

Left A doctor treats a boy with a distended stomach. Under the leadership of such famous physicians as Hippocrates of Cos (presumed author of the Hippocratic Oath), Greek medicine made great advances towards a scientific attitude, attempting to base its diagnoses on observation, aided by diets, purges and emetics.

Below left This fragmentary scene represents the lying-in-state of a young Athenian woman who has died unmarried. She is wearing a crown, as if for her wedding. Behind, a relative is tearing her hair in grief. The woman on the right is a slave, revealed as such by her cropped hair. The vase itself is a *loutrophoros*, a vessel especially made to mark the graves of those who died unmarried.

Below An Athenian gravestone. The dead woman, whose name was Hegeso, is seated on a chair while her maidservant hands her a jewel-box as she says farewell. Many such gravestones, with sculptured reliefs of family and friends bidding farewell to the deceased, have survived from the 5th and 4th centuries BC.

COMPANIONS OF THE DEAD

Ancient Chinese tomb figurines

Tomb robbers are the villains of archaeology, as indefatig-able in their efforts to find and disperse tomb treasures as the archaeologists are in seeking to preserve them. As we have seen, they penetrated all the great pharaonic tombs of Egypt, except that of Tutankhamun, and rifled many splendid Etruscan chamber tombs, depriving posterity of many valuable relics. They also despoiled nearly all the visible imperial tomb mounds of China, from that of the First Emperor and unifier of China, Shih Huang Ti (died 210 BC), to those of the very recent Manchu emperors. But in one case they played an unexpectedly constructive part. Of all the imperial mounds, 13 tombs of the Ming emperors (dating from the 15th to the 17th century) had escaped robbery, no doubt because of their proximity to Peking. When in 1957 the government decided to excavate just one of these, that of Wan Li (1573–1620), certain tomb robbers, in jail for rifling the more remote Manchu tombs, were paroled to give the archaeologists "expert" advice on how to find the tomb chamber itself, which in all the imperial burials was cleverly hidden within the huge mound. Combing the wooded top of the mound, the robbers pointed out a tree that had tilted because of earth subsidence over a concealed shaft. The shaft led down to another shaft, and finally into the tomb itself, which was filled with undisturbed treasures – priceless porcelain, jade vessels on golden mounts, magnificent jewelry, ingots of silver and gold. Presumably the helpful robbers were returned to jail. Another, much earlier robber of a T'ang tomb suffered a different fate. Apparently killed by his

colleagues, perhaps as an informer, his skeleton was found by archaeologists in 1964 at the inner end of a tunnel dug by the robbers into the tomb of the Princess Yung T'ai (706 AD), who according to history was either flogged to death or forced to commit suicide by her terrible grandmother, the Empress Wu. The robbers had stolen most of the tomb's precious objects but had left behind, as valueless, hundreds of charming clay figurines, some of which are illustrated on the following pages.

The building of royal tomb mounds, from that of the First Emperor to recent times, is typical of the extraor-dinary continuity of Chinese culture over some 2,000 years. The huge mound of the First Emperor, a brutal tyrant, still exists, but was plundered in antiquity and has not been excavated, though a collection of thousands of lifesize clay statues of his imperial guard, perhaps portraits, was recently discovered by chance close to the mound. According to tradition the emperor's childless wives were killed and buried with him, and all the tomb workmen were enclosed alive in it. The custom of burying figurines of clay (and sometimes bronze) with the dead to serve them in the afterlife began in the Han period (206 BC–220 AD) and reached its apogee in the T'ang dynasty (618–906 AD). It is thought to have replaced human sacrifice, which was certainly the royal practice in Shang times (the first known dynasty, c. 1500–1027 BC). The custom slowly declined and was replaced much later by large-size figures of paper which were burned at the funeral. "Warlords" of modern times had whole paper armies, including cavalry, artillery and airplanes, burned at their burials.

If the First Emperor unified China within its now traditional boundaries, the Han dynasty, which came to power a few years after his death and lasted for over 400 years, made it an empire. Han exploring parties and finally whole armies marched south towards Vietnam and west to the shores of the Caspian, discovering to their astonish-ment not only India and Persia but the Roman Empire. During the 53-year reign of the Emperor Wu (141–87 BC), shaper of this new empire, wealth and learning increased

Opposite above Lifesize pottery figures being excavated from burial pits near the tomb of the First Emperor, who died in 210 BC. His huge tomb-mound is at Lint'ung, near Sian in Shensi province. Altogether over 5,000 such figures, comprising a complete army with its horses, were unearthed. A special museum in Peking is being constructed especially to house them.

Below Painted wooden figures from the tomb of the Lady T'ai, an aristocrat of the Han Dynasty, whose grave (1st century BC) was found near Ch'angsha in Hunan province. The figures were stacked in the cavity between the outer and inner coffins of the tomb.

and a vast bureaucracy developed to handle its affairs. The recent discovery of several tombs of the 2nd and 1st centuries BC has illuminated the splendor and sophistication of this period – notably that of Prince Liu Sheng, a brother of the Emperor Wu, and his wife Tou Wan, both of whose bodies were encased in suits of jade sewn with gold thread; and the tomb of an aristocrat, Lady T'ai, whose body was found almost intact, along with well-preserved food offerings, sumptuous silk embroideries, porcelain and jade. After this time the custom grew of placing in the tombs clay models and figurines intended to perpetuate the objects and scenes of everyday life, especially the magnificent "celestial" horses acquired after 101 BC from western Asia. These became status symbols for the privileged classes as is shown in the famous Han bronze horse-figurines of over a hundred years later, found in a tomb in 1969, which included the incomparable "flying horse."

The use of tomb figurines of surpassing naturalism and variety came to a climax in the 8th century AD under the T'ang, when China had become the greatest and most sophisticated empire in the world. Many hundreds of figurines, some of them glazed, were placed in the important tombs like that of the Princess Yung T'ai, portraying the servants, retainers, favorite activities and fine horses and carriages of the deceased, and even camels loaded with the exotic goods coming from Asia. There are complete village scenes, groups of women playing polo, elegant, wasp-waisted and elaborately costumed court ladies, huntsmen, acrobats, musicians and entertainers. The figurines reflect above all, in their preoccupation with the portrayal of foreigners, the cosmopolitan atmosphere of the capital, Ch'angan, probably the largest city in the world, where one could see Turks, Arabs, Asiatics, Indians, Cambodians, Koreans, Negroes, Greeks and Syrians. The T'ang was China's golden age and was never surpassed.

Below Two pottery tomb figures dating from the Han dynasty. They probably represent attendants or minor officials. One has his hands tucked behind a sash.

Opposite Two pawing and neighing "celestial" horses excavated from an Eastern Han tomb at Wuwei, Kansu province, in 1969. Dating from the 2nd century AD, this tomb was a major find, containing no fewer than 177 bronze objects, including the famous "flying horse." About 15 inches tall, these horses are superbly naturalistic pieces of sculpture, beautifully executed.

Left A female pottery figure, about 25 inches high, found in 1964 near the tomb-mound of the First Emperor Shih Huang Ti at Lint'ung, near Sian, Shensi. This appealing figure probably represents a servant, buried in an offering sanctuary at the approach to the imperial tomb.

Right A troupe of pottery acrobats, tumbling to the sound of gongs and a drum, found in a Western Han dynasty tomb (2nd–1st century BC) at Tsinan, Shantung province. Acrobats were popular as entertainers in China.

Above and **right** Figures from the tomb of Princess Tou Wan who lived in the late 2nd century BC. The tombs of the princess and her husband Liu Sheng, a member of the Han imperial family and prince of Chungshan, were excavated in 1968. Cut deep into a hillside at Manch'eng, Hopei province, they had never been robbed, and yielded fabulous treasure, over 2,800 items in all, including the princess's remarkable jade suit, which has been reconstructed. The leopards above are only about 1⅓ inches high. They are made of bronze, partly gilded and inlaid with silver and garnets. They were probably used to weigh down the edges of the funeral palls. The two grotesque figures on the right are a pair of feet from a bronze vessel. About 4½ inches high, they represent bears rearing up on the backs of two rather unhappy-looking birds. Both the superbly crafted leopards and the bears were probably personal possessions rather than tomb effigies.

Left Another bronze model from the tomb excavated at Wuwei (see previous page). The horse (about 16 inches high), carriage with sunshade, and attendants are on the same scale as the other horses. The efficient breast-strap harness indicated (the actual harness has disappeared) was a late Han development.

Right A spirit guardian cast in earthenware, found in a grave of the North Ch'i dynasty (late 6th century AD). Such figures, reflecting popular religious beliefs, were placed in tombs to repel evil spirits.

Far right Pottery figures of two women, probably attendants or concubines. They date from the Northern Wei dynasty (6th century AD).

Right A warhorse made of pottery, complete with harness and trappings. It comes from a tomb of the Northern Wei dynasty (6th century AD). The narrow nose and head is the typical style of the period.

Opposite A band of itinerant musicians from Central Asia sitting on the back of a camel, who appears to be making a loud protest. This remarkable figure, dating from the 7th or 8th century AD, is typical of the tolerant, cosmopolitan attitudes of the great T'ang empire.

Right Items from the T'ang tomb of Princess Yung T'ai, who died in 706 AD. According to historical accounts she was either forced to commit suicide or flogged to death by the tyrannical Empress Wu, her grandmother; but an inscription in the tomb, excavated in 1964, says diplomatically, that she died in childbirth. **From left to right** are a horse and rider (probably a groom from Central Asia); a group of horses, guardians, grooms and soldiers placed just as they were found in a niche built into the wall of the tomb; a finely modeled pottery horse; and (**below, far right**), a mounted hunter, again a Central Asian, with his hunting cheetah – a T'ang custom known from literature. All of these figures represented the servants, retainers and animals of the deceased.

Below The seated figure of a woman, T'ang dynasty, glazed and painted. She may have been an entertainer, holding a musical instrument (now lost) in her hands. From Shensi.

Right A camel and its attendant, found in a tomb near Sian, Shensi province, in 1959 (T'ang dynasty, early 8th century AD). The bearded attendant is probably a trader from Central Asia. The camel's saddle is curiously ornamented with a bearded face, and is loaded with vegetables and other items.

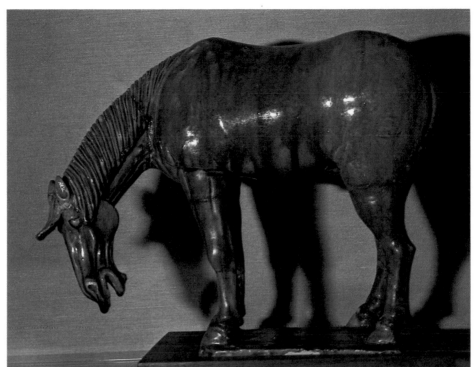

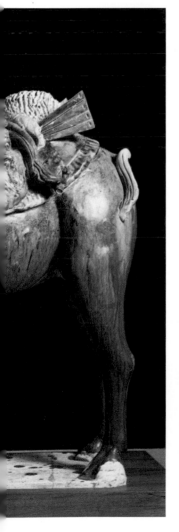

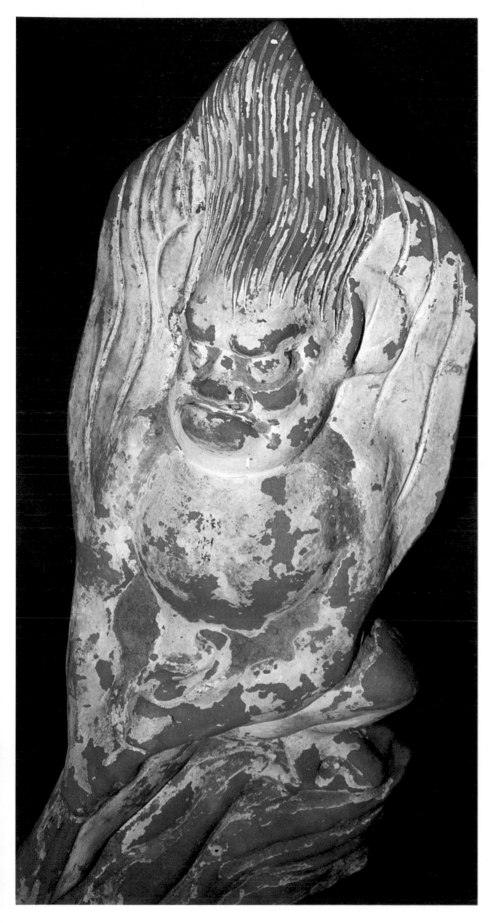

Above A fashionable lady of the T'ang dynasty, with long sleeves of the type still worn on the Chinese operatic stage when traditional T'ang sleeve dances are performed.

Left A guardian figure from a tomb of the T'ang period. Like the grotesque figure on a previous page, it was thought to protect the dead from evil spirits. Similar terrifying figures were placed in niches at the entrances to Buddhist temples.

Opposite A T'ang glazed pottery figure of a cross-eyed wineseller with his leather wine bottle. He is a westerner, possibly an Armenian, one of many representations of westerners found among T'ang period tomb figures.

CERVETERI

Etruscan tomb art

In 1848 George Dennis published a classic book on the Etruscans, whom he described as "people of mysterious origin and indefinite antiquity." Perhaps he was inadvertently responsible for the aura of mystery which popularly surrounds the Etruscans. In fact a great deal is known about the Etruscan culture, largely owing to the discovery of tombs, like those of Cerveteri, in which the Etruscans attempted to re-create (like the ancient Egyptians) a facsimile of their life on earth for the comfort of the dead. But the origin of the Etruscans is still a mystery, and so is their language. The language can be "read," because it is written in Greek letters, but not much of it can be understood, for it appears to belong to an ancient pre-Indo-European language with few parallels. Etruscan died out as a written language in the 1st century BC, and the once-extensive Etruscan literature is almost entirely lost. Some 10,000 inscriptions in Etruscan are known, but most are short funerary or religious texts. Hence the Etruscans, though they left a wealth of visual remains for the archaeologist to study, are mute: they cannot tell us about themselves, and much of what we do know comes from the writings of their enemies, the Greeks and Romans. As to their origin, Herodotus in antiquity said they came from Lydia in Asia Minor, an idea which is still taken seriously because their art and culture are so obviously based on those of the eastern Mediterranean, and especially the Greek. But this could as easily be explained by an indigenous people trading with those regions from earliest times and absorbing their culture, a theory which now begins to look more likely.

Indigenous or not, the Etruscans created their impressive culture in Italy, and the final mystery is why, when they seem to have had every chance of dominating

Italy if not the entire West, they lost out to the Greeks and Romans and were forgotten for over 1,500 years. At their height, from 600 to 500 BC, their cities extended from the Po valley down to the region of Naples. Their immense wealth was based largely on the export of metal ores and metal products, and they were skilled craftsmen, traders and sailors. They built fine roads and bridges, diverted flood waters through underground channels and equipped their cities with sewage systems. Above all they developed a most attractive and distinctive culture, earthier than the Greek but always lively. From the evidence of the tomb paintings they never did anything by halves, throwing themselves with abandon into feasting, dancing, music-making, horse racing, sports and hunting, with their women often as partners, unlike the Greeks. They were famous, too, for their obsession with religion, which was originally joyous but in the days of their decline turned dark and fearsome.

The Etruscans, in a loose federation of cities, began their climb to power when Rome was a collection of hut villages on the Seven Hills, and Greek and Phoenician traders and colonists were disputing the western Mediterranean. They not only held these easterners from their shores but grew rich on their trade while competing with them on the seas – often siding with the Carthaginians (of Phoenician extraction) against the encroaching Greeks. Some Carthaginians lived peaceably at Pyrgi, the port of Chaire (Latin Caere, modern Cerveteri) and, about 535 BC, fleets from there joined Carthaginians in wresting Corsica, opposite the Etruscan coast, from hostile Greek colonists. During the 6th century (traditionally from 616 BC until 510 BC), the Etruscans ruled Rome itself and nursed it into a great city. Then in the 5th century the tide turned. The Greeks, who had already stopped the Etruscans' southward thrust, gained control of the seas from them in a naval battle in 474 BC. In the 4th century, while the Gauls attacked from the north, the Romans, as they grew stronger, reduced their cities one by one, beginning with the great city of Veii, only 12 miles from Rome, which they utterly destroyed in 396 BC after a 10-

Opposite above One of the large burial mounds in the Banditaccia cemetery at Cerveteri. Up to about 130 feet across, the largest of these tumuli sometimes contain several burial chambers.

Below Gold beads found with the body of Larthia in the Regolini-Galassi tomb at Cerveteri. They are decorated with finely incised designs.

year siege. Roman persistence, and the inability of the Etruscan cities to unite in the face of danger, spelled the end. But Rome the destroyer, ironically, borrowed much of its early culture from the Etruscans.

Today it is hard to avoid the mania for anything to do with Tutankhamun, but Etruscomania is far older, reaching back over 200 years, ever since fine bronzes and superb Greek vases began to turn up in tombs discovered by accident. Soon the amateur scholars and the cranks had begun to belabor the "mystery" of these strange people, inaugurating a flood of printed works on the Etruscans which has never ceased to grow. By the 19th century the "excavating" of tombs for treasure, either by robbers or by fine gentlemen like Lucien Bonaparte, Napoleon's brother – both were equally destructive – had become widespread. Much damage was done, but fortunately there were thousands of tombs and many of them were well hidden. In recent years the development of new methods of detection has enabled the archaeologists to keep ahead of the robbers. Aerial photographic surveys, developed during the war, have revealed many tomb fields, and devices such as the proton magnetometer are

then used to locate the tomb on the ground, after which a scanning camera, invented by Carlo Lerici, is inserted into the tomb to see if it is worth opening. The magnificence and variety of objects recovered from the tombs over the years have naturally encouraged extremely competent faking, so that many eminent museums have recently been embarrassed when their finest Etruscan exhibits have been declared to be forgeries.

After 650 BC Cerveteri, lying about 30 miles northwest of Rome near the coast, became the leading manufacturing city of the Etruscans, making and exporting metalwork, gold objects and fine *bucchero*, the black Etruscan pottery. Like all Etruscan cities it was surrounded by cemeteries, among them the Banditaccia, lying to the northwest, and the Sorbo, the oldest, on a plain to the southwest. The Sorbo contained the early Regolini-Galassi tomb, first opened in 1836. The first chamber tombs were cut into the rock under circular tumuli topped with rubble; the later ones were rectangular constructions built along "funerary avenues"; but all the tombs show us what domestic houses, complete with their furnishings, looked like on the inside between the 7th and 5th centuries BC.

TREASURES FROM THE
REGOLINI-GALASSI TOMB
Found in 1836 in the Sorbo cemetery, this
tomb dates from about 650 BC and is named
for its discoverers. It contained some of the
richest treasures ever found in an Etruscan
tomb. One of the occupants of the tomb was
cremated, and his ashes were placed in the
fluted funerary urn (**below right**). The lid-
handle in the shape of a horse is an imitation of
a style of Greek Geometric pottery. The cremated man was obviously a warrior, for his war-
chariot (**below left**) was placed in his tomb
with him. It was originally made of wood with
bronze cladding, and enough metal fragments
survived to make a reconstruction possible.

The magnificent gold breastplate (**right**),
$16\frac{1}{2}$ inches high, belonged to one of the three
people buried in the tomb, a woman named
Larthia (her name is known because it is
inscribed on a bronze vessel found among her
grave goods). The breastplate, with its
intricate stamped decoration, was sewn onto
the garment in which Larthia was buried. All
this luxury was paid for by extensive trade in
bronze and iron ore with the Aegean area.

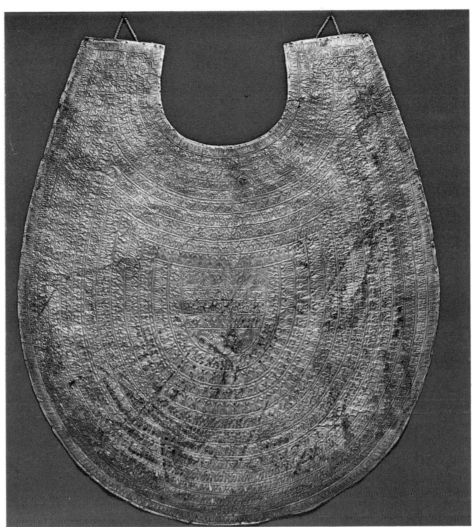

ETRUSCAN TOMB INTERIORS
The Tomb of the Capitals (Tomba dei
Capitelli) in the Banditaccia cemetery at
Cerveteri (**above**) dates from the early 6th
century BC. It consists of a large room
supported by two octagonal columns, and
three smaller rooms. Such a tomb no doubt
reflects the interior of an Etruscan house of the
period. The deceased were laid out on the
stone-cut funerary couches, one of which can
be seen in the picture.

The Tomb of the Reliefs (**right**), also in the
Banditaccia cemetery, is later, dating from the
4th century BC. It is decorated with stucco
reliefs of armor, weapons and household
goods. In a broad stone bench in front were no
fewer than 32 burials, all members of a family
named Matuna, as inscriptions indicate. The
principal niche in the center, carved to look
like a couch with pillows and ornamental legs,
held two persons, probably the same principal
members of the family whose effigies, now
defaced, adorned the columns on either side.
The reliefs below the couch represent the
monster Typhon with snakes for legs, and
Cerberus, the three-headed guard dog of the
underworld.

The inner chamber of the earlier Regolini-
Galassi tomb in the Sorbo cemetery is shown
far right. This tomb contained three burials
and rich treasures, some of which are shown
on the surrounding pages.

Many of the tombs near other Etruscan
cities have magnificent fresco wall paintings.

Below A *bucchero* flask found in the Regolini-Galassi tomb with an Etruscan inscription in Greek letters, and a Greek alphabet around the base. The flask has been useful in the attempt to interpret the Etruscan language.

MORE TREASURES FROM THE
REGOLINI-GALASSI TOMB
One of the most remarkable finds was a large
ornamental gold fibula (a clasp or safety-pin),
over 12 inches long (**opposite**), found in the
inner chamber with Larthia's burial. The
lower plate has rows of tiny ducks swimming
up it. Equally exquisite were two gold
bracelets with relief panels, also belonging to
Larthia. The upper relief of one (**left**) shows a
woman standing between two stylized palm
trees, flanked by a pair of lions; each lion in
turn is being stabbed by a man. In the lower
panel three women alternate with three palm
trees.

The wooden cart (**below**), reconstructed
from surviving metal fragments, was found in
the outer chamber of the tomb. With its
bronze bed, it was probably used in the
funerary procession to convey the body of the
dead person to the grave.

THE BOYNE VALLEY TOMBS

Prehistoric graves in Ireland

Huge stones, incredible numbers of them, are still standing in sites all through western Europe, despite the ravages of untold centuries. Nearly 50,000 megalithic monuments of many types are scattered from Spain to the Orkneys, from Scandinavia to Ireland. They range from stones standing singly or in marching files of thousands, as in Brittany, to the great stone circles of England, including Stonehenge. But the majority are tombs of various types, like the passage graves of Ireland. The monuments are so old that until recently their origin could only be guessed at. Myths and legends gathered around them, and the Christian Church from its earliest years, sensing their pagan origin, tried to break them up, or neutralize them with a cross or convert them to chapels. Yet until recent times peasant girls danced around the stones in an echo of ancient fertility rites whose meaning they scarcely knew. If people wondered what they were, they most often assumed, as was widely thought to be the case with Stonehenge, that they were the work of the Druids. But today, thanks to careful archaeological investigation and study, we know that these tombs and monuments are indeed the relics of a remote age, the Neolithic – an age that was inventive and progressive, though without writing or even the use of metal – and that they were built over a period stretching from about 4500 BC to 1500 BC at the dawn of the Bronze Age. This is a span of time as long as from the present back to the biblical King David.

Until recently it was supposed that the megalithic builders learned their art from the more civilized Mycenaeans of the Aegean. There was a marked resemblance, for instance, between the megalithic passage graves of western Europe, with their corbeled burial chambers, and the handsome corbeled tombs of the Mycenaeans, such as the famous Treasury of Atreus at Mycenae. Some thought that actual colonists from the Aegean had introduced the art to Spain, whence it had spread northwards, and that later on Aegean craftsmen may even have helped build Stonehenge 3. But the megalithic monuments, according to the latest corrected radiocarbon dates, are now found to be mostly older than their supposed Aegean prototypes. Of these, the monuments in Brittany rather than in Spain are now thought to be the oldest – around 4500 BC. Stonehenge is now dated about 2000 BC and the Boyne Valley passage graves in Ireland around 3000 BC. The magnificent, many-chambered temples and tombs of Malta, once thought to be of Aegean inspiration and an example of the megalithic "spread" to western Europe, are now found to be older than the Aegean monuments and probably bear little relation to the megalithic monuments in general. Though the transmission of ideas, particularly what might be called cultic practices, from one country to another is not ruled out, monument building in most areas seems to have been largely of local growth, a stage everywhere in the development of the Neolithic rather than the spreading of a culture. However, there has been much debate as to whether or not the Boyne Valley graves reflected influences from the somewhat earlier but rather similar corbeled passage graves of Brittany.

Despite great variety in details, the megalithic monuments fall into several general groups: the menhirs, or single standing stones (some are as tall as 70 feet); the circles or long straight lines of menhirs, as in England and Brittany; and the dolmens, or roofed tomb structures. The simplest of the tombs have a single small chamber; the more elaborate collective tombs are subdivided into gallery graves, in which the whole tomb consists of a long covered chamber; and the passage graves. The latter, including our Irish examples, have a long, stone-built passage leading into the burial chamber or chambers; these sometimes have a corbeled, or false-vault roof. The whole is set under a large mound, or tumulus. Graves of this type are found in Spain, Portugal, Brittany,

Opposite Excavation of the prehistoric cemetery at Knowth. The archaeologists have cut neat sections out of the main mound, revealing the construction layers and the large curbstones around its perimeter. Curbstone 43 (**below**) was decorated with the typical curved lines and circles of Neolithic ornament.

Scandinavia, Ireland and the Scottish highlands and islands (for example the splendid Maes Howe tomb on Orkney). The labor and organization that went into the construction of these huge monuments by simple Neolithic farmers reminds one of the dedication shown by the builders of the Egyptian pyramids, or the medieval cathedrals; for undoubtedly these collective tombs were not only "houses for the dead," built for eternity, but also ritual centers for a whole tribe or region.

The finest passage graves in the British Isles are those in the Boyne Valley, particularly the huge tumuli of Knowth and New Grange. The former is the largest and most elaborate, the latter is slightly smaller but is distinguished by its unique wealth of geometrical incised decoration – Neolithic symbols with magical or religious meaning which also occur on similar tombs in Brittany and Spain. Little is known about these monuments beyond a few intriguing facts. The megalithic burial ritual lasted in Ireland for some 500 years, but in these tombs only a chosen few were buried over the centuries. Who were these special people? Kings? Priests? Soothsayers?

Probably the latter, people with supernatural powers who could predict the movement of the sun, moon and stars and thus help to establish a yearly calendar. For country people are always sensitive to the pattern of movement in the skies above them, and Neolithic farmers had to know when to sow their crops or they would starve. Stonehenge was a kind of astronomical observatory, and so was New Grange at least among the passage graves; for at New Grange uniquely there is a slot or "roof box" above the door and every year precisely at 8:58 am on December 21 – the winter solstice – the rising sun strikes through the box to illuminate the 70-foot passage right into the burial chamber at its end. The brilliance lasts for 17 minutes and then gradually fades as the sun continues rising in the new-year sky. This dramatic means of marking the shortest day of the year can hardly be a coincidence. Moreover there is evidence that New Grange, and probably other tombs, with their circles of standing stones and smaller satellite graves, were laid out on careful geometrical principles. These tombs were the cathedrals of the day.

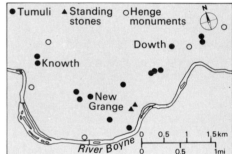

Above Sketch map of the chief monuments in the Boyne Valley in Eire, about 25 miles north of Dublin. Knowth and New Grange are the largest and most important sites. New Grange, widely known for its unique decoration, was excavated earlier; Knowth is still under investigation.

Left Aerial photograph of the excavation of the main mound at Knowth, nearly 300 feet in diameter, taken in 1968. The mound is systematically stripped by making a box grid of trenches. At least 16 smaller tombs have been found close around it.

Above The eastern passage in the main mound. It leads into a more elaborate cruciform chamber with corbeled roof and side chambers.

Left The terminal chamber of the western passage tomb in the main mound. The construction is simple: upright slabs, with capstones across the top.

Below left An ornamental stone basin found in a side chamber at Knowth. The mound is unusual in containing two graves, with the longest passages known in Europe respectively 108 and 111 feet long.

Below One of about 16 smaller passage graves excavated around the perimeter of the main mound at Knowth.

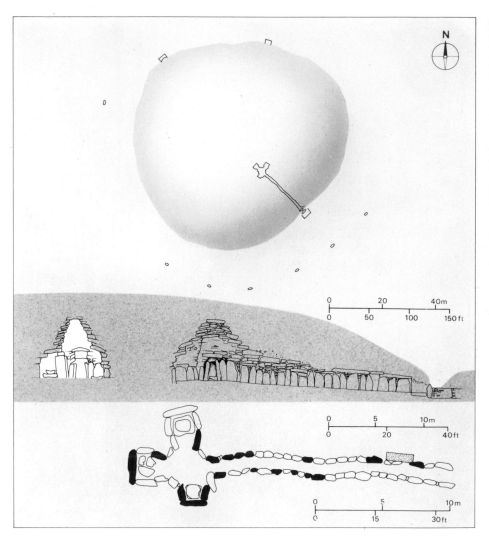

The famous mound of New Grange lies less than a mile away from Knowth. Almost equal in size, it contains some 200,000 tons of stone, but covers only a single passage grave. As indicated in the diagram **right**, the passage ends in a cruciform chamber with a corbeled roof, in which each layer of stones projects slightly above the lower one until they meet in the middle, forming a cone.

Below Aerial view of the mound at New Grange. Originally the mound was surrounded by 35 standing stones, 12 of which survive and can be seen in the foreground, and in the diagram at right.

Below right As at Knowth, an ornamental stone basin was found in the chamber at the end of the passage at New Grange. These basins probably contained the ashes of the "special people" buried in the mounds.

Above The richly ornamented curbstone standing before the reconstructed entrance to the passage at New Grange. A mark at the upper middle of the stone centers the complex geometrical layout of the mound and its satellite graves. Above the doorway is the unique slot or "roof box" which was closed except at the winter solstice, when the rising sun shone into the passage right to its end.

Right Spiral ornament on one of the uprights inside the passage at New Grange. The ornament at New Grange is the richest of its kind in Europe, rivalled only by certain tombs in Brittany (with Ireland, one of the two chief centers of megalithic art). This abstract geometrical art is found mostly in passage graves, and not in all of those. It must have had symbolic or ritual significance connected with the megalithic burial cult.

Right Looking straight up into the corbeled roof of the burial chamber at the end of the New Grange passage. The progressive overlapping of the stones to form a cone can be seen. The major passage graves were considered "houses of the dead" and were even carefully waterproofed so that, like the Egyptian tombs, they would last for eternity.

THE EGYPTIAN PYRAMIDS

Monuments of the early pharaohs

The Great Pyramid of Gizeh is still the largest man-made structure in the world. It covers 13 acres, was once some 480 feet high, and except for the internal passages consists of solid stone blocks throughout – nearly 2,500,000 of them weighing on the average $2\frac{1}{2}$ tons apiece. It was built about 4,500 years ago, near the dawn of Egyptian civilization, by men whose tools were of copper and stone, who lacked lifting devices and the wheel, and who inched these huge stones into place by means of rollers, inclined planes and the lever alone. Yet even by today's standards the precision of its north–south orientation and of its engineering is astonishing.

There has been much fanciful speculation. Following after Piazzi Smyth, the brilliant but eccentric Astronomer Royal for Scotland and the pioneer pyramidologist of the 1860s, a host of wide-eyed zealots have poured out untold books and pamphlets purporting to prove, with a curious mixture of mathematics, mysticism and religion, that the Great Pyramid was designed by means of a lost hermetic science, more advanced than anything known until modern times; that it was a scale model of the Western Hemisphere, an observatory, an oracle predicting the future, a compass, a vast theodolite, or even, in its unfinished state, a landing site for extraterrestrial visitors. It has even been maintained that there was a mystic geometrical significance in the triangular loincloths traditionally worn by the pharaohs! It is also a widely-held article of belief that nobody knows for certain when the Great Pyramid was built, for whom, or why.

All this theorizing deliberately discounts over a century of devoted work by the Egyptologists, whose findings clearly indicate that the Great Pyramid was built as a funerary monument for King Khufu (Cheops) of the 4th dynasty, and that it dates from around 2600 BC. The development of the pyramid can also be traced, from the prehistoric pit burial up to the *mastaba*, a mud-brick

superstructure erected over the grave with separate chambers for the possessions. The *mastabas* then become larger and more elaborate, suggesting in their architecture the palaces of the living; and at this point a genius named Imhotep enters, one of the earliest recorded examples of an individual who has swayed history. Prime Minister to King Djoser (Zoser) of the 3rd dynasty (c. 2685 BC) Imhotep was long remembered in antiquity as an architect, mathematician and physician. First he took a decisive step in building his master's *mastaba* of stone instead of mud-brick. Not content with this, he gradually extended and rebuilt it, first into a four-step stone pyramid, then into the magnificent "Step Pyramid" of six steps at Saqqara which can still be seen today. To keep this earliest skyscraper from falling down, Imhotep cleverly built it up with a series of inward-leaning, vertical buttress walls, the outer ones providing the steps. The next advance came with three pyramids, all probably belonging to Sneferu, the first king of the 4th dynasty, whose successor was Khufu of the Great Pyramid. The first one, at Meydum, was a disaster. According to a delightful and plausible study by the eminent physicist, Kurt Mendelssohn, the builders tried to make it into the first true pyramid by filling in the steps, but the outer mantle and casing, being poorly bonded to the steps, collapsed when the building was nearly finished – accounting for the 250,000 tons of limestone which now lie around the base of the strangely truncated pyramid. In an effort to avoid another disaster, the next two pyramids, at Dahshur, were given odd profiles. Both are true pyramids, but the angle of elevation of the "Bent Pyramid" curiously decreases part way up, while the "Red Pyramid" is built entirely at the lower angle, giving it a squat appearance. So the superb engineering of the next, the Great Pyramid, was not achieved by means of some lost hermetic science but through painful trial and error. Quite a few pyramids are scattered up and down the Nile Valley, but the great age of pyramid-building lasted at the most only a few hundred years. The few pyramids built subsequently were small and shoddily constructed.

The pyramidologists do have a point when they ask:

Opposite The sheer size of the Great Pyramid of Gizeh is dramatically displayed in this closeup of one corner. Each stone weighs about $2\frac{1}{2}$ tons. The pyramid originally had a facing of polished limestone.

why all this prodigious labor just to build a royal tomb which was not even proof against the grave robbers? The pyramids *must* have had some other, esoteric purpose ... The Egyptologists have an answer to this too. We have already seen an example of a simple agricultural society mobilized to build a massive structure, as at Stonehenge. The early Egyptians regarded their pharaoh as a god incarnate. He was their protector, and the fate of every Egyptian depended upon his continued existence after death in a tomb that would endure for ever. The attempt to create such a tomb culminated in the building of the great pyramids, and this required the mobilization of almost the entire population, not as slaves but as work gangs toiling to ensure their own salvation, like the laborers and craftsmen who built the Gothic cathedrals. In

the 4th dynasty pyramid-building became an obsession. And this involvement of the whole country had an unexpected result. Not only did it keep the idle peasants busy during the flood period, but it brought about the creation of a large and efficient bureaucracy and corps of experts, all under the control of a powerful centralized government – in other words it helped to transform a primitive rural society into the first real nation state. By the end of the 4th dynasty, however, the status of the pharaoh had subtly changed. He was no longer considered a god, but merely the son of a god – the sun-god Re'. If he was less of a divinity in his own right, he was now a powerful head of state – and the need for vast pyramid-tombs was no longer felt. Thus the pyramids marked the coming-of-age of Egyptian civilization.

Below The precursors of the pyramids were the very early pit burials covered by a mound (left). These were followed by the *mastaba*, a chambered burial place with a mud-brick superstructure, shown in plan and cross section in the diagram below.

Bottom An artist's reconstruction of King Djoser's Step Pyramid (right), earliest of the pyramids, with its complex of buildings around it enclosed within a wall with 14 false doors and only one real entrance. Its gifted architect, Imhotep, was later deified.

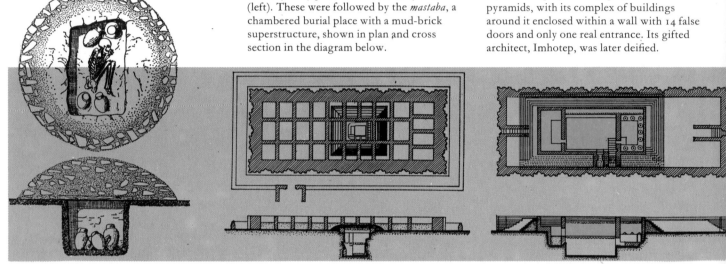

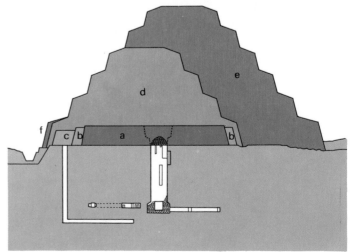

Above and **right** The Step Pyramid at Saqqara, built by Imhotep for King Djoser after 2700 BC. The diagram on the right shows the stages in its construction. It started off as a typical *mastaba* (**a**) only 26 feet high, though built of stone, to which a facing of limestone was added (**b**). It was then further enlarged on the east side (**c**), forming low steps. It was next built up into a four-step pyramid (**d**), like four *mastabas* on top of each other. Finally the pyramid was enlarged again to the north and west to form the six-step pyramid whose remains are still standing. It rose to a height of 204 feet, and was encased in limestone. Underneath can be seen the burial chamber and passages. Here was the beginning of the Egyptian pyramid.

Left The pyramid at Meydum that probably collapsed. It may have begun as a *mastaba*; it then became a step pyramid, finally a true pyramid. But the outer casing was poorly bonded to the steps and collapsed, with some of the steps, leaving only the core.

Below The "Bent Pyramid" at Dahshur. Built by King Sneferu of the 4th dynasty, it represents the next advance towards a true pyramid shape. In order to prevent a repetition of the disaster at Meydum (so one assumes), the builder designed the top half of the pyramid at a shallow angle, giving the whole monument a "bent" appearance. There is evidence that Sneferu was building three pyramids at once, one probably as a tomb, the others as cenotaphs, or memorials to the king.

Left Closeup of the "Red Pyramid" at Dahshur. This was the first true pyramid, but as can be seen very clearly in this photograph, the architect was still "playing safe" and constructed the pyramid at a very shallow angle (43° 36′ instead of 52° in the famous true pyramids at Gizeh).

Below The pyramid of King Khafre (Chephren) at Gizeh stands as a backdrop to the Great Sphinx, which bore his face and was part of his pyramid complex. This included, in addition, a mortuary temple, a valley building, a causeway connecting the two and five boat pits.

Overleaf The great pyramids of Gizeh. The largest, the Great Pyramid of Khufu (Cheops), stands in the background. In the center is the slightly smaller pyramid of Khafre (Chephren), while the pyramid of Menkure (Mycerinus), less than half the size of the other two, is in front. The pyramid of Khafre still has some of its Tura limestone casing at the top. In the foreground are three minor pyramids. Note the step construction of some of them. Cairo lies in the distance beyond the Nile.

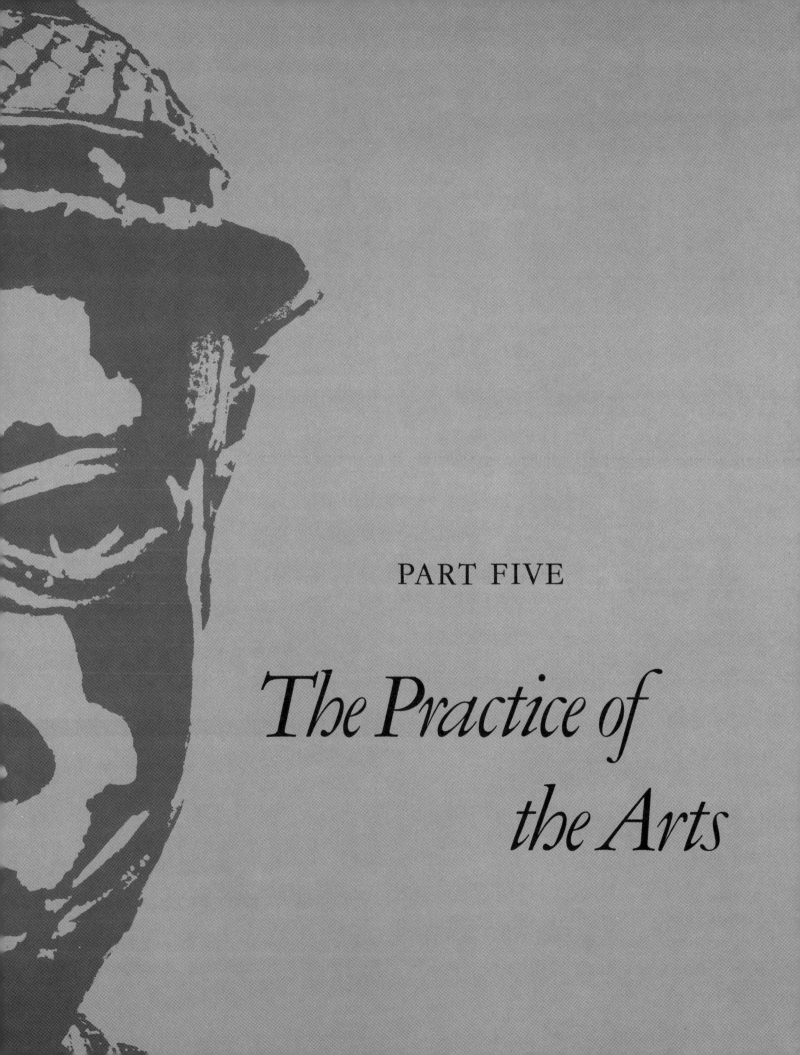

PART FIVE

*The Practice of
the Arts*

CHINESE LANDSCAPE PAINTING

Art and reality

There is something immensely attractive about Chinese civilization. From the earliest times the Chinese kept always before them an ideal of harmony, of tolerance and decency, of unity and a respect for tradition to which, after each period of anarchy or division in their long history, they unfailingly returned. The Chinese were earthy and pragmatic, shunning metaphysics as well as religious bigotry and dogma; yet their almost spiritual love of beauty and of nature was infused with a mystic feeling for the harmony of a man within himself, and of man with nature. This was most perfectly expressed in the art of landscape painting, one of China's greatest legacies to the world, which developed rather late in her history, during the expansive T'ang period (618–906 AD) and rapidly reached a first, magnificent flowering during the more restrictive, inwardlooking Sung dynasty (960–1279 AD) which followed. Seldom has there been a more sophisticated and subtle art than this. The landscape paintings of the early Sung masters, like those of Fan K'uan and Kuo Hsi, are symbolic and philosophical in meaning. They celebrate the majesty of nature in which man and his works – the winding path, the bridge, the inconspicuous thatched cottage and man himself almost lost in the grandeur – have their humble place. For man is happiest if he conforms to nature, to the "way" of Taoism; on the other hand nature must be rational, balanced, orderly, as Confucius taught, in harmony with man as the virtuous man is in harmony with nature. Then there is the Buddhist surrender to the totality of nature. There is something of all three systems in these paintings, a curious mingling, in Western terms, of the rational and classic with the romantic. The scholar-painter, while at court, might be the most correct of Confucian bureaucrats, but when he retired to the country to paint he was swayed by a mystical

feeling of unity with the power of nature which owed much to Taoism and even to Ch'an (Zen) Buddhism.

But to the painter it was the work itself that really mattered most, and here a subtle grouping of techniques quickly brought landscape painting to an early maturity. The scholar-gentleman's tool was the brush, which could be used equally for the fine art of calligraphy or for painting (both were based on the skilled manipulation of line), or for the writing of poetry, for the three were closely related, and beautifully calligraphed poems were often brushed onto the paintings to enhance them. Traditionally, the artist painted either on a vertical hanging scroll, which suited the tall grandeur of the mountain landscapes, or on an album leaf, or on the horizontal handscroll which could be slowly unrolled to reveal a sequence of related compositions, moving forward in time and space like a piece of music with its related movements. Indeed the Chinese felt that a landscape should show country that is good to walk in – here a path, there a bridge, an inn or a lake. One should be able to travel through a painting, like *The Red Cliff*, a handscroll in which the eye travels down the river from the near foreground on the left into receding distance on the right, or the famous Sung painting *Streams and Mountains without End*, a seven-foot handscroll depicting a path which not only wanders from right to left through extremely varied scenery but which also moves from one style to another of six of the most revered Sung landscape painters. Depth in a landscape was obtained by subtle fields of mist separating foreground from background. The artist usually sketched from nature – preferably the dramatic, craggy mountain scenery of the south and a few other regions – but he composed his complex work in the studio, as one can see if the paintings are matched with actual landscapes.

Little has been preserved of early Chinese painting, mostly wall paintings from the Han tombs (206 BC–220 AD) and painting on tiles and pottery. By late Han times the use of the brush was well developed, and during the Six Dynasties period (220–580 AD) the first master painters

Opposite *Early Spring* by Kuo Hsi (dated 1072 AD), a hanging scroll in ink and light colors on silk by an early Sung master. Their favorite subject was the rugged and precipitous mountains of parts of China. In this picture the only signs of human activity are the tiny figures (bottom, left and right) and the village (right background).

and art treatises appeared. In the meantime Buddhism had entered China, bringing from the West enriching elements of Classical, Indian and Persian painting which led, by the T'ang period, to a widespread school of brightly-colored Buddhist wall and scroll painting. Through the 9th century figures predominated, both in painting and sculpture – including the famous T'ang figurines (see pp. 175–9 above). But landscape painting developed rapidly during the T'ang, and this led to the first great flowering of landscape painting under the early Sung, which set a pattern for the future – for Chinese painters, while seldom merely imitating, assiduously copied the old masters in order to learn from them and, incidentally, to preserve them. The Sung emperor Hui Tsung, who lost his life and his throne when the Tartars overran north China in 1125, founded the first academy of painting in the Orient and was himself a talented painter and collector (*Autumn over Hills and Rivers*, reproduced here, is attributed to him). The scholar-painter now came into his own, the gifted

amateur who after the Sung court had fled south from the Tartars, preferred to work for himself rather than for the conquerors in the north. Thereafter Chinese landscape painting developed with incredible vigor, diversity and increasing sophistication up through the subsequent dynasties – the conquering Mongols, the Mings, the Manchu (Ch'ing) – to at least 1800 AD when it began to lose its impetus. Styles proliferated, some delicately calligraphic, some monumental, others suggestive or deliberately spontaneous, and near the end some almost "expressionistic" landscapes appeared which today seem amazingly modern. But all this brilliant diversity was securely based on the masterpieces of the early Sung, which remain unsurpassed.

Below A scene in southern China, at Yangsu near Kueilin, Kuangsi province. The mountain pinnacles are as steep and fantastically shaped in reality as they are in so many of the landscape paintings they inspired.

Left A very early Chinese mountain landscape in a fresco from the Caves of the Thousand Buddhas, Tunhuang, Kansu province, dating from the T'ang period (618–906 AD), when Chinese landscape painting began. It depicts the Buddhist pilgrim Hsüan Tsang returning from India. The precipitous mountains that feature in the later tradition are already in evidence in the foreground.

Above *The Red Cliff*, attributed to Wu Yüan-chih (c. 1195 AD), a detail of a Sung handscroll, ink painting on paper. The Red Cliff is an actual spot on the River Yangtze, near Wuchang, although less dramatic in reality than the artist's imagination has made it.

Left Boats on the upper Yangtze river, in a grim and imposing gorge that lacks some of the romance of the painting. The bare rocks mark the level of summer flooding, when meltwaters come down from the Himalayas.

Far left *Travelers among Mountains and Streams* by Fan K'uan (early 11th century), a detail of a Sung hanging scroll, ink and colors on silk. Man's proper relation to the overwhelming power and grandeur of nature is emphasized by the diminutive travelers in the foreground, humbled by the huge mass of the mountain above them.

Center Some landscapes in China are scarcely less dramatic than those of the artists. Here herb gatherers scale a pinnacle on Mount Huangshan in the northwest, amid scenery that has all the elements of classic landscape painting: precipitous crags, clinging trees, deep valleys, swirling mist.

Right *Literary Gathering in a Mountain Lodge*, by the Ming artist, Wang Fu, a hanging scroll, dated 1404. Almost 400 years after Fan K'uan the same tradition is flourishing, showing the strength and continuity of landscape painting in China, owing in part to unremitting copying of the classics.

Right and **above** Once again the strange dreamlike and mysterious quality of a Chinese landscape painting has its basis in real Chinese landscape. The painting is *Autumn over Hills and Rivers*, attributed to the Emperor Sung Hui Tsung (12th century AD), a hanging scroll in ink and light color on paper. The phenomenon of pinnacles floating in mist can actually be seen in the photograph above, taken at sunrise in the southern mountains. The seals on this and other paintings are those of collectors and owners.

Opposite Archetypical Chinese landscape – the famous limestone pinnacles of southern China, again at Yangsu near Kueilin. Very little change would be needed to make this scene a typical landscape painting – the figures would become smaller and the mountains would tower more dramatically.

THE BUDDHA

Images in painting and sculpture

Until recently the arts of Indian Asia were an enigma to the West. The stylized, cool abstraction of many of the Buddha figures, contrasted with the wild exuberance and frank sexuality of much of the rest, perplexed and even repelled people in the West. Though an inspired artist like Rodin deeply admired the Indianized sculpture of Southeast Asia, a more general opinion was voiced by Sir George Birdwood, an English art critic, in 1910. Referring contemptuously to a Javanese Buddha figure as "vacuously squinting down its nose to its thumbs, knees and toes," he added: "A boiled suet pudding would serve equally well as a symbol of passionate purity and serenity of soul."

Today the arts of Indian Asia, so alien to Western eyes, are beginning to be recognized as a direct and vigorous expression of the impressive range of Indian thought and religion; indeed, they seem almost indistinguishable from Indian civilization as a whole, which during its great period between 500 BC and about 1200 AD spread widely over much of Asia, building a series of Indianized kingdoms in Southeast Asia and profoundly affecting the cultures of Central Asia, China, Korea, and Japan. This was one of the world's major civilizations, extending almost 2,000 years in time and stretching geographically from Afghanistan on the borders of the Middle East to the Philippines, from tropical Java to the barren wastes of Mongolia. And it was certainly the religious and philosophical content of this civilization, based on a set of ancient symbolic ideas condensed into two sacred and thus unalterable national literatures, that gave it its strength and tenacity and made it so attractive to the many races and cultures of Asia. The great parallel literatures which formed the content of the Indian arts were the Hindu Veda and the literature of Buddhism. Though they were quite different from each other, as Hindu art is often different from Buddhist art, each played its part in the spread of Indian civilization, helping to colonize Asia at different times and in different places; in fact it is sometimes difficult to disentangle the two, since both shared much the same mythic and religious Indian background.

The images of Buddha, the subject of this chapter, are but one small aspect of this greater Indian whole. Buddhism developed almost side by side with Hinduism, which grew out of the older, caste-based Aryan religion; but Buddhism was a more personal religion with a savior figure, like Christianity. The Buddha himself, born about 567 BC as Siddhartha Gautama, a prince of Nepal, became an ascetic and after his enlightenment under the Bodhi tree began to preach a message of salvation through worldly renunciation and the gradual attainment of Nirvana. His was a spiritual faith open to all and without a god or any set worship. But soon after Gautama's death it quickly developed into a fully-fledged religion, propagated by monks. It was later espoused by the powerful Mauryan emperor Ashoka (272–232 BC) who also introduced it into Sri Lanka, whence it spread to Burma and Thailand. The typical Buddhist structure was the *stupa* or pagoda, a mound originally intended to hold relics, the earliest of which are to be found at the Buddhist centers of Sanchi in central India and Sarnath on the Ganges. Buddhism fostered large monasteries such as the rock-cut complexes at Ajanta and Karli in west-central India. By the 1st century AD both Buddhist and Hindu colonies, following the active inland and maritime trade routes of the day, had appeared in Southeast Asia – Java, Sumatra, Malaya, Cambodia and the coasts of Thailand and Indochina. At the same time in India the Kushans, nomads from Central Asia, conquered an empire in northwest and central India and thereafter, from their capitals in Gandhara, now in Pakistan, and Mathura in north-central India set the pattern for much of the later art of both Hindus and Buddhists. Controlling the east–west trade routes

Opposite above This striking Buddha comes from Nepal, Buddha's homeland. It is part of a page from a Wisdom manuscript written on a palm leaf in the 10th century AD.

Below The Buddha, according to tradition, was born from his mother's side, as shown in this relief from Gandhara in Pakistan (2nd century AD). Gandharan sculptors, who were the first to produce Buddha images, were much influenced by Greco-Roman art.

between Rome and China, they grew immensely rich, and, as fervent Buddhists, used their wealth to build and adorn shrines and monasteries in a curious half Greco-Roman, half Indian style which eventually formed the basis for the Buddhist arts of China, Korea and Japan. In India Buddhism continued to flourish through the golden years of the Gupta dynasty (4th to 6th centuries AD) but thereafter declined in the face of an ascendant Hinduism, which had absorbed much of its ethical content, and finally disappeared. In China, similarly, it gave way to Confucianism after the 10th century; in Java it produced, before its eclipse, the huge *stupa* monument of Borobudur (c. 800 AD). But in parts of Asia Buddhism still flourishes – in Burma and Thailand, for instance, and in Japan, along with the native Shinto religion (see pp. 251–59).

Perhaps because of the asceticism of the original faith, no images of Buddha were made for some 500 years after his death. Nor is Buddha himself shown on the delightful carvings of his legendary life on the gates of the 1st-century AD Great Stupa at Sanchi. Instead, he is represented by symbols such as a throne or a cushion, a wheel, a pair of footprints or the Bodhi tree. But as

Buddhist doctrine was elaborated, it was finally agreed that a body of Buddha could be portrayed – not his physical body, nor the indescribable body of total enlightenment, but a symbolic body representing the tranquil spiritual status of the great teacher. This is the meditative, seated Buddha thereafter common throughout the world. In its developed form it has the symbolic protuberance of wisdom on top of the head, a tuft of hair between the eyes, the wheel or lotus marks on hands and feet. The doctrine also held that the Buddha nature, although one and indivisible, could also manifest itself in an infinity of individual Buddhas reflecting different aspects of the deity, often indicated by the position of the hands. The first images of Buddha appeared, strangely enough, under the foreign Kushan dynasty in Gandhara and especially in the great art center of Mathura, which supplied the impetus for all later images, Buddhist or Hindu. Since the Kushans were heavily influenced by Greco-Roman art, the idea of the Buddha image may have arisen under them from a fusion of existing Indian sculptural traditions with the example of Greco-Roman deities such as the sun god, Apollo.

Above Buddha the ascetic. This 2nd-century AD stone image from Gandhara represents the extreme asceticism practiced by the Buddha before he received enlightenment under the Bodhi tree. He later rejected asceticism as a means of discipline.

Right The Buddha shown symbolically. It was many centuries before the followers of the Buddha began to represent his figure, and in this limestone relief from Amaravati in southern India (2nd century AD), the Buddha is symbolized by two cushions on a throne under the Bodhi tree. He is being attacked by Mara, the god of death.

Top left A meditating Buddha carved in the pure Gandhara style, 2nd century AD. It comes from Taxila in Pakistan, and belonged to a monastery built by the Kushans, nomads from Central Asia, who created a wealthy Buddhist empire based on trade.

Above The Buddha sitting in the "Lotus" position. The gestures of the hands indicate that he is teaching. This sculpture in the Gupta style, dating from the 5th century AD, comes from Sarnath on the Ganges River, where the Buddha preached his first sermon. Images of this type were extensively exported to the Far East and Indonesia, or were copied there.

Top right A brooding Buddha with two attendant Bodhisattvas, or holy Buddhist figures, in one of the 5th century caves of the great rock-cut monastery of Ajanta in central India. Ajanta's 27 caves were carved and decorated with wall paintings for over six centuries, from the 1st century BC.

Above left An elegant seated Buddha of terracotta, from the now-vanished *stupa* of Mirpur Khas in Pakistan, 4th century AD. It was originally painted and formed part of the facing of the monument. The *stupa*, whether free-standing or carved deep in caves such as those of Ajanta, was the typical Buddhist monument. It was originally intended to hold relics.

Above right A standing Buddha of the Gupta style (5th century) from Mathura in northern India, once a capital of the Kushans. The sculpture of Mathura, in the typical local pink sandstone, was a model, with that of Sarnath, for the Buddhist sculpture of Indian Asia.

Far left An ivory figure of the Buddha from Kashmir, 7th century AD. The Buddha is being tempted by the opulent daughters of Mara, the god of death, whom he eventually overcame by his discovery of the true way of enlightenment.

Above Teaching Buddhas painted on the wall of Cave 2 at Ajanta, 6th century. The multiple images represent the very Indian idea of an infinite number of universes and therefore an infinity of Buddhas appearing to teach enlightenment.

Left A free-standing colossal bronze figure of the Buddha from Sultanganj in India (9th century AD). It dates from the Pala period (8th to 12th centuries), the last flowering of Indian Buddhism before it was swept away by the Muslim conquerors. Superb bronzes like this were typical of the period.

Left A huge meditating Buddha at Gal Vihara in Sri Lanka (Ceylon), dating from the 12th century. The conservative style of the image, derived from India, is typical of the "fundamentalist" Hinayana Buddhist school which dominated the island.

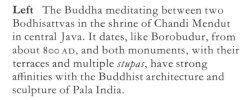

Above A seated Buddha, other-worldly in its feeling, meditates eternally on a terrace of the immense temple mountain of Borobudur in central Java. The monument was built about 800 AD by a Shailendra king, and fell into disuse about 1000 AD.

Left The Buddha meditating between two Bodhisattvas in the shrine of Chandi Mendut in central Java. It dates, like Borobudur, from about 800 AD, and both monuments, with their terraces and multiple *stupas*, have strong affinities with the Buddhist architecture and sculpture of Pala India.

Above left The Buddha dying and passing into Nirvana. This colossal figure, cut into the rock face at Polonnaruwa in Sri Lanka (Ceylon), represents a type of reclining Buddha frequently repeated in later centuries in southern (Hinayana) Buddhist countries.

Above A 12th-century stone carving of the Buddha from the Thai city of Ayutthaya. Sculpted in the style of the Hindu Khmer kingdom of Cambodia (see pp. 38–45), it represents the Buddha meditating, seated on a magical *naga* or snake. In Buddhist legend a *naga* once saved the Buddha by raising him on its coils above the floodwaters sent by Mara, the god of death. In Khmer mythology the *naga* was also a symbol of cosmic fertility.

Left This huge gilded image of the Buddha dates from the 13th century and represents a type of Buddha image that was first created in the city of Sukhodaya in Thailand. Most Buddha images in all countries were originally gilded like this one. Buddhism was known in all of Southeast Asia but flourished most strongly in Burma and Thailand.

Left A meditating Buddha image (which is still venerated) sitting among the ruins of a shrine called Prang Sam Yot in the ancient Thai city of Lopburi. Behind is a *stupa* very reminiscent of the architecture of Angkor Wat (see above, pp. 38–45) which, however, was inspired by Indian Hindu rather than Buddhist concepts. Hinduism and Buddhism existed side by side in Southeast Asia and their styles were often very similar.

Below left and **below** Two images of the Buddha in the smooth and sinuous style developed at Sukhodaya, a center of Buddhism in Thailand in the 15th century. The reclining figure represents the dying Buddha passing into Nirvana, and the upright figure of a walking Buddha is on a votive tablet. Buddhism, which was diffused through Southeast Asia by well-educated monks, is still the state religion of Thailand.

Above left and **left**   The Buddha in China. This remarkably
preserved, delicate embroidery (9th century AD) comes from the Caves
of the Thousand Buddhas in Tunhuang, Kansu province, an entry
point in the far northwest for Buddhism, which spread east along the
caravan routes from India. The subject is "The Buddha preaching on
the Vulture Peak." The lower figure is one of the rare early Buddhist
works in the far south of the country. Buddhism was strongest in the
north and spread from there to Korea and Japan.

Above and **right**   The Buddha in Japan. The wooden gilded image
(**above**), almost 10 feet high, is in the ancient Byōdō-in temple in Uji
near Kyoto. It is the masterpiece of the renowned sculptor Jōchō,
who worked for the Fujiwara in the 11th century. The colossus
(**right**), also 10 feet high, is the largest dry lacquer statue in Japan,
made by chinese monks in the 8th century for the Tōshōdai-ji temple,
Nara.

IFE AND BENIN

Early African sculpture

The African sculptures of Ife and Benin, in southern Nigeria, are remarkable in three ways: their exceptional quality, their antiquity, and the fact that they were created by what we like to think of as a primitive people. The best of these sculptures date from our Middle Ages and earlier, yet their artistic quality compares favorably with that of the world's great schools of sculpture. These are not the usual wooden masks and other carvings from Africa, rightly called primitive, whose powerfully abstract forms greatly influenced Picasso and other artists in the early 1900s. The later sculptures of Benin are often stylized, but the best of the Ife heads are elegantly classical in feeling, so much so that Leo Frobenius, a German scholar who came to Africa in 1910, thought they must somehow have been derived from the art of ancient Greece.

Ife was in decline when the Portuguese arrived on the Guinea coast in 1471, but Benin was a powerful state, and its school of sculpture was still flourishing in the early 17th century when a Dutchman described its straight main street as "seven or eight times broader than the Warmoes street in Amsterdam," while the king's palace alone "occupied as much space as the town of Haarlem." But by 1897, when a British punitive expedition entered the town, it was sadly decayed. The troops found its streets littered with bodies, sacrificed by the Oba to his gods in a vain attempt to ward off the British evil. Before burning the city to the ground the troops wantonly looted a wealth of carving and sculpture in brass and bronze, for in those days few cared anything about African art.

Frobenius was one of the first to make an investigation of the sculpture of the Yoruba region of Nigeria. He sank deep shafts in a sacred grove outside Ife and discovered marvellous terracottas and bronzes, "the remains of a very ancient and fine type of art." But he refused to admit that the sculpture of Ife was of local origin, and in the end decided that it must be a relic of the civilization of the lost island of Atlantis! One remembers the ruins of Great Zimbabwe in southeastern Zimbabwe, which to this day are still thought by some to be of Phoenician or Egyptian origin (see pp. 26–31).

Fortunately much is now known about Africa's neglected and colorful history. There is, for instance, much documentation from Arab and European sources relating to the large medieval trading empires of Ghana, Mali and Songhai in the western bulge of Africa. Growing wealthy on the caravan trade from North Africa, they flourished from about the 5th to the 16th centuries AD. The greatest and richest of the Mali emperors, Mansa Musa, went on pilgrimage to Mecca in 1324 and on his way distributed so much largesse in gold in Cairo that he disastrously upset the local money market! There is much less documentation, except for Benin perhaps, on the smaller kingdoms of the rain forest belt along the southern coast of the bulge, which probably also benefited from an extension of the caravan trade down to the coast. There is even less information on Ife, which never became a kingdom; and by the time the Portuguese arrived it had lost all power, though it continued to be revered as the spiritual center of the Yoruba people. Benin, however, flourished within recorded history. It still has a royal brass-casting industry, and Benin traditions insist that the knowledge of metal-casting came originally from Ife.

Archaeology, with its related disciplines, is a fledgling science in Africa. Recent discoveries have greatly extended the probable age of the Nigerian sculptural tradition. These include the Nok terracotta figures, sometimes nearly lifesize, belonging to a widely extended culture of the earliest Iron Age, as well as the remarkable hoards of intricately embellished bronze objects of all sorts found in a grave and shrines at Igbo Ukwu. Radiocarbon dates suggest a range for the Nok culture from as early as 500 BC up through the first centuries AD, and for Igbo Ukwu from the 8th to the 10th centuries AD and probably

Opposite above Guards flank the entrance to the Oba's palace at Benin, and a python symbolizes his power. Portuguese heads adorn the palace columns.

Below Oldest of West African sculptures, this terracotta Nok head is some 1,500 years older than the Benin bronze plaque above.

beyond. Ife reached its high point between the 10th and
14th centuries AD, and Benin during the 15th to 17th
centuries.

This chronology, together with strong stylistic and
technical similarities between the arts of the four periods,
suggests an impressively long and unified tradition for the
sculpture and metal-casting of the Nigerian forest. But
modern scientific research must move slowly and
carefully, and nothing is yet certain, not even, despite
tradition, any definite connection between Ife and Benin,
while recent excavations, supplemented by stylistic studies
and analyses of metals and of casting techniques, have so
far brought out as many differences as similarities between
the arts. However, ritual motifs such as snakes and
leopards recur in most of the forest arts, which again
suggests continuity. Much of the Ife sculpture, like that of
the Nok, was in terracotta; of the metal figures a few were
in copper or bronze, but most, like those of Benin, were in
leaded brass. The "lost-wax" method of casting was used
by all the West African metalworkers, though even here

there were differences between the techniques used at Ife
and at Benin. Benin's metal guilds always worked for the
royal court. Plaques covered the pillars and beams of the
palace, and lifesize heads adorned the shrines, all
commissioned by the Oba. It is tempting, but unwise, to
suggest that the same occurred at Ife, although the arts
may have been practiced for the court as well as for other
purposes. For instance, most of the 14th-century terracottas shown in the following pages came from an outlying
farm, and were all dedicated there in a single local shrine.
Whatever the truth, we may enjoy this unique art for its
own sake – the delicate spirituality of some of the Ife
sculpture contrasted with the earthy vigor of the Benin
brasses.

Below These fine bronze castings from a shrine at Igbo Ukwu
(8th–10th centuries AD) attest to the antiquity of Nigerian metal-
working. The openwork cylinder depicts a woman with facial
scarifications (11 inches high). The decorated bowl (top right) imitates
a calabash gourd, and the vessel below it represents a marine triton
snail surmounted by a leopard.

Top Two views of an Ife terracotta head (half life-size) found in a shrine, along with other sculptures and a group of human skulls, at a site outside Ife called Obalara's land. The head portrays malevolence and horror.

Above This superb copper mask has long been kept in the royal palace at Ife. It is the only surviving Ife mask and is said to portray Obalufon II, the third Oni of Ife. The head is pierced to attach hair and beard to it. The wearer looked out through slits under the eyes.

Right A rare Ife "bronze" – in fact it is made of brass – found in 1957 on the outskirts of the old town of Ife. Nineteen inches high, the figure is thought to represent an Oni, the Yoruba king of Ife. He holds a magic horn in his left hand.

Above A standing figure from the Obalara shrine (15 inches tall), one of a pair found buried together. The large head and short body are characteristic of much African sculpture.

Above right Another terracotta head from the Obalara shrine. The tall hat closely resembles the traditional crowns of Yoruba kings.

Right This magnificent bronze, 20 inches high, makes an interesting comparison with the Ife figures. It comes from Tada, north of Ife on the Niger river, and is one of 11 bronzes preserved there in shrines.

Far right An Ife head that looks much like an individual portrait. From the Obalara shrine.

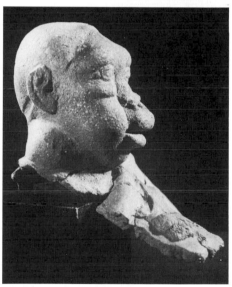

Above and **top right** The head above, with its serene beauty, is the classic Ife type. The face was once painted red and the eyeballs white. The striations on the face may be an attempt at modeling, whereas those on the other head (**top right**) probably represent the elaborate facial scarifications of Ife. Both come from the Obalara shrine.

Left A pot from the Obalara shrine, found with the skulls, portrays cult objects – a snake and a standing leopard (both symbols of royalty in Benin) and a human sacrifice in the form of a decapitated head, gagged with a rope to stifle curses. A leopard's head also forms the pot's mouth. A similar pot portrays three terracotta heads in an open, roofed shrine, suggesting how the Ife heads were used.

Above This sickly creature, with bleary eyes, a running nose and goiter, was found at the Obalara shrine with the human skulls, the pot depicting human sacrifice and two more heads, one the obese creature showing an expression of horror. The style of these figures (their bodies are lost) is totally different from the serenity of the classic Ife type and seems to be associated with rituals of death and sacrifice. The Ife terracottas were reverenced and carefully preserved even when broken.

Left Benin statuettes portraying royal messengers from Ife, the Yoruba spiritual center, showing typical facial scarifications.

Right Head of an Oba from Benin, probably from a later period (17th or 18th century) and cruder and heavier than the earlier style.

Below A Benin statuette of a Portuguese soldier. Benin maintained friendly trading and diplomatic relations with Portugal from 1486 for over 100 years, until the Dutch took over.

Below right One of the many courtyards in a contemporary Yoruba palace in western Nigeria, with traditional sculptures of kings and deities in place. Such courtyards are the scene of regular ceremonies and sacrifices.

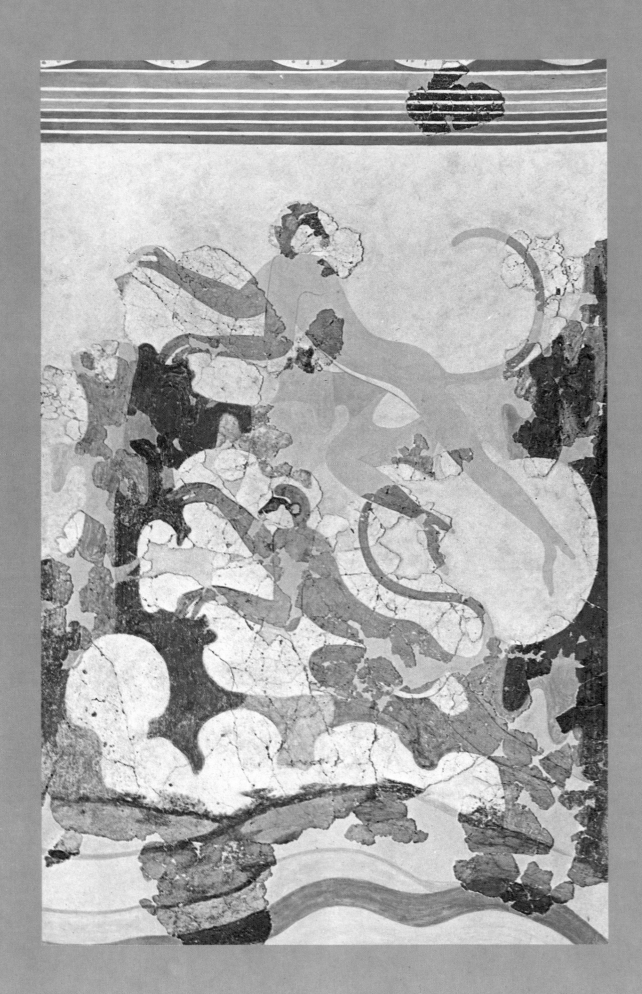

FRESCOES FROM THERA

A Minoan settlement uncovered

The rise and fall of the rich Bronze Age civilizations of the Aegean – the talented Minoans of Crete giving way later to the warlike Mycenaeans of Greece – is, as we have seen, one of the most dramatic and tantalizing stories in ancient history. Curiously intertwined with this history is the effect of the volcanic explosion of the Aegean Island of Thera (now Santorini) about 1500 BC. One of the most stupendous eruptions in history, it tore the mountain island apart, leaving only a deep sunken crater, now a lagoon, rimmed by the scattering of smaller islands one sees today. In Bronze Age times the island, only 70 miles north of Crete, was a Minoan colony, and with its fertile volcanic soil it was heavily populated. The remains of at least two settlements, apparently established about 1550 BC, have been found beneath the heavy layers of ash that now cover the islands. One in particular, at Akrotiri, excavated from 1967 by the Greek archaeologist Spyridon Marinatos, has revealed parts of a Minoan town, its streets and houses remarkably preserved beneath the infiltrating ash. Its extent is not yet clear. Among the rich and varied finds at Akrotiri, the paintings on the walls of many of the houses are outstanding. Not only are they the most complete Minoan frescoes ever found, but they are also of surpassing beauty and great historical interest. Akrotiri is another Pompeii. But there is a difference: the inhabitants of Thera somehow had warning of the impending disaster and fled, carrying with them their most valuable and portable possessions.

The Thera explosion has an even wider meaning in Aegean history, for its date, 1500 BC, neatly divides the two main periods of that history, the Minoan and the Mycenaean. When the island was overwhelmed, Minoan Crete was at the height of its power and glory and its ships and its culture dominated Greece, the Aegean and beyond. But shortly after the explosion its power waned and the renascent Mycenaeans from the mainland began to take over, and finally, as the archaeological evidence seems to show, conquered Crete itself. Was there a connection between the catastrophe and the fall of Crete? Most scholars now think there was, but until recently there was much controversy about the details. The difficulty was that Crete's palaces and villas were destroyed in a general holocaust about 1450 BC, half a century later than the explosion of Thera. Nevertheless some scholars still tried to connect the two, although the destructions of 1450, which extended to areas that could hardly be reached even by the power of such an explosion as that of Thera, appeared rather to be the result of a hostile invasion. Today, after intensive investigations by archaeologists, vulcanologists and other specialists, a consensus begins to emerge. In particular, the remarkably similar explosion of the much smaller island of Krakatoa in Indonesia in 1883 has been studied for its lessons. Krakatoa's big bang killed 36,000 people and was heard 2,000 to 3,000 miles away. Thera's much vaster explosion, preceded by earthquakes and lesser eruptions, which may have alerted the islanders, spewed forth large chunks of pumice and a huge blanket of volcanic ash which blotted out the sun for days and drifted halfway to Egypt, as seabed core analyses have made clear. Eastern and central Crete was covered by a fallout of perhaps four inches of ash; but this, with the tidal waves and earthquakes, still does not explain the destructions of 1450 BC. It now seems more likely that the Minoan civilization of 1500 BC, with its elaborate bureaucracy and luxury-loving upper classes, was already somewhat over-extended and thus fragile. After the explosion the Cretans would have been terrified and demoralized by the darkness, the earthquakes, the poisonous fumes and falling ash, and the great tidal waves lashing the coast after the sea had rushed back into Thera's empty crater. With their ships destroyed by the waves, their trade interrupted, and their land poisoned by the blanket of ash, perhaps for a generation, the Cretans must have been so weakened that 50 years later the Mycenaeans, now in the ascendant, were able to take Knossos and from

Opposite The "Blue Monkeys," although sadly damaged, is one of the most lively and dramatic of the Theran frescoes. The complete fresco portrays a whole pack of agile monkeys sweeping in a continuous frieze around two walls of a house.

there ravish and subdue the rest of Crete. For in 1450 BC Knossos alone was scarcely damaged, and from the archaeological evidence the Mycenaean presence in the palace thereafter is quite clear.

And so the explosion of Thera sealed the Akrotiri settlement, as in a tomb, at the very peak of Minoan achievement. (Indeed, this island that sank into the sea may be the original Atlantis, later mistakenly placed in the Atlantic.) True, there are local traditions at Thera intermixed with the Minoan, for the Cycladic islands, of which it is one, had previously produced their own variation of Aegean culture, marked by the lovely marble figurines of the Early Bronze Age which are now so admired. But by 1500 BC the islands had come almost completely under Minoan influence, and thus the paintings and objects found at Thera are basically Minoan, though with some local themes. The frescoes of Thera are far better preserved than any from Crete itself, but both reveal the sheer exuberance of Minoan painting. It was an art of movement, of outline, catching in a few deft lines the feel of an animal in motion, the grace of a woman's body, the shape of a flower, as befitted the fresco technique which required rapid painting on the drying plaster. There was nothing solemn or monumental about Minoan art; and one may be sure that the civilization it reveals was just as ebullient, as sophisticated as the art itself. It was a civilization in which color, action, enjoyment were prized for their own sakes, in which women seem to have been almost as free as men, a civilization which was sociable and relaxed. The Thera frescoes tell us much about this civilization we did not know. Both the Minoans and the Mycenaeans were great sea-traders, roaming the Mediterranean, and here we see their actual ships at sea, gaily bedecked and painted. We see modern-looking towns, the landscapes of the Aegean, boys at sport, and above all the elaborately-gowned, confident, graceful women of this brilliant society.

Below Thera is still an active volcano. Smoke and steam is seen rising here from the eruption that took place in 1926 on the small islets in the middle of the ring of islands that surrounds the sunken crater.

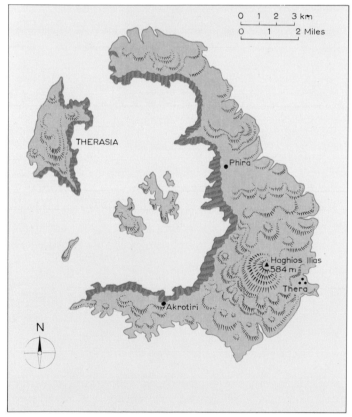

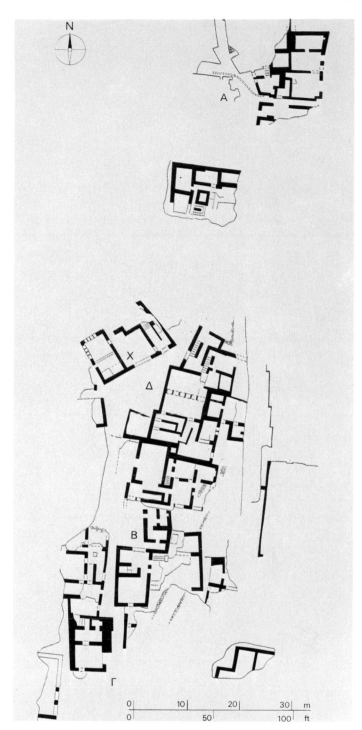

Top The town of Phira lies on the top of the dramatic red cliffs which form the inside walls of the crater made by the great explosion of 1500 BC.

Above Thera today. The huge lagoon in the center, surrounded by a ring of cliffs, marks the sunken *caldera*, up to 1,400 feet deep, formed when the great eruption blew the center out of the island. Rich Bronze Age houses have been excavated on Therasia, while a whole town is being unearthed at Akrotiri. It is at Akrotiri that the finest frescoes have been found.

Above Plan of the Minoan settlement being excavated at Akrotiri. Like Pompeii, it was buried under a thick layer of volcanic lava and ash. The whole township and the finely built houses are similar to others found at sites on Crete such as Zakro and Palaikastro. The houses marked B, Δ and X contain the frescoes illustrated on these pages. The excavations have not yet revealed the extent of the ancient town. No large public buildings have been found, though it is not impossible that a palace, in the Cretan manner, may lie buried somewhere nearby.

Left Spring flowers and birds. This delightfully exuberant fresco occupied three sides of a small room in the house marked Δ on the plan on p. 233. It is the best-preserved of all Aegean frescoes. Others, as on Crete, have been laboriously reconstructed from fragments. The large flowers appear to be some kind of lily.

Below A procession of ceremonial ships setting out from a town gives a rare glimpse of the kind of craft used by the seafaring Minoans. This remarkable scene, which appears to be placed in North Africa, is part of a fresco over 20 feet long found in house X, named the "House of the Admiral." It is eloquent testimony to

the wealth, sophistication and widespread trading contacts of these accomplished people. Note the lavish decoration and long thin bowsprits of the ships.

Above Part of a frieze of antelopes which decorates three sides of a room in house B. The Minoans took delight in depicting birds and animals.

Left The south wall in the same room as the antelopes on the previous page was decorated in an unbroken frieze with these two young boxers. Each one wears a single glove and a girdle. The bracelets and jewelry on one of them and their well-coiffured hair indicates that these are privileged youngsters. They are depicted with all the verve and movement of the Minoan artist.

Right This elaborately dressed woman with her flounced over-skirt, golden earrings and painted cheeks was one of three female figures adorning a room of one of the larger houses with staircases and many rooms. This room was probably a shrine and the women priestesses are shown presenting a seated goddess with a robe.

STONE AGE ART

Painting and sculpture of early man

The best of Stone Age art – notably the paintings in the great cave-sanctuaries of France and Spain and the sculptured figures – can be compared with confidence to the best of human art in any period of history up to the present. Yet this art was created around 15,000 years ago – well outside history as we know it – by a school of artists who belonged to the earliest true men (*Homo sapiens*) on earth. There were no antecedents for this art since the Neanderthals, the not quite-human hominids who preceded these early so-called Cromagnon men, seem to have had no art at all. This suggests that art has been, from the very beginning of our species, an innate expression of our humanity. This school of art – and it was a school, like those of ancient Greece or the Italian Renaissance – flourished like most such schools in a definite area, centering on France. From small beginnings it was slowly nurtured to the level of sophistication illustrated on the following pages. Some scholars, noting the many loose pieces of stone or bone covered with doodles or sketches found in the caves, suggest that there may even have been "studios" of prehistoric art. This Upper Paleolithic school lasted, not hundreds but thousands of years – from perhaps 30,000 BC to 11,000 BC.

Of course over such a period of time different styles and techniques evolved, with local peaks and troughs. There were at least four cultural stages: the French Aurignacian, Perigordian, Solutrean and Magdalenian, with the Eastern Gravettian roughly paralleling the later stages in the west. Offshoots can be identified in Spain, Italy, Sicily and Europe to the east, extending well into Russia. But there is an underlying unity to the whole period and a gradual forward progression up to the high point of Middle Magdalenian art. After 10,000 BC there is a rapid falling off as the Ice Ages ended, the climate warmed, the herds of

game animals moved north and the whole magnificent culture of the Ice Age hunters collapsed. Curiously enough, it was the very rigors of the Ice Ages that produced this culture: the bleak, frozen plains roamed by vast herds of animals, the cruel climate that drove men to take shelter where possible in caves. Their entire culture as well as its art was focused on the animals, predominantly reindeer in the west, mammoth in the east, which provided their food and clothing, and the bone, ivory and antlers to make (along with stone) their weapons, tools and even their jewelry. Except for the occasional edible plant, they were almost totally dependent on animals, and in turn the animals gave them a good life. Like the Eskimos, they had managed to achieve a fine adjustment to their environment and consequently were tough, resourceful and intelligent. They lived in well-built shelters at the mouths of their caves or in the open. Their sophisticated equipment included delicate bone needles and probably crude lamps for heat and light. They were skilled hunters for meat which they ate or stored. They dressed well and warmly, buried their dead decked out in all their finery; and with plenty of leisure between hunts, there must have been time for elaborate ceremonies with dancing and music, as well as for the practice of the arts.

The repertoire of the Stone Age artist included carving or modeling in the round, lines engraved with a flint burin, or engraving tool, raised relief and, finally, painting. These seem to have developed roughly in that order, though often several different techniques were used together. Sculpture seems to have reached an early climax with small animal figures, and especially the amply endowed female figurines, the "Venuses," which are found from France to Siberia. Paint was first applied to engravings in the caves, then often used in its own right. The colors were derived from natural earth pigments, carried in little bone tubes, and were applied with the fingers, a brush or a mouth spray. Reds, browns, blacks and yellows were used, but apparently not blue and green. All these techniques culminated in the impressive Magdalenian "art galleries" in the French and Spanish

Opposite Detail from a large panel of paintings (see next page) in the famous cave at Lascaux, in southwest France. The ox has been painted on top of two smaller figures of a deer and a horse. The horns are drawn in "twisted perspective," as if seen head on, a common convention in cave art.

caves, though from the beginning small movable objects of all kinds – spearheads, harpoons, pendants – were elaborately decorated. The gifted Magdalenians in particular exuberantly decorated everything they could lay their hands on. In painting, no perspective was used, but the artists had learned to shade with skill.

What was the purpose of this art? Why were the cave figures placed one on top of another in an apparently random fashion? Why were some of the scenes painted far in the interior of the sanctuaries, like Altamira in Spain and Lascaux in France, where they could not be seen? Some profess to see large-scale "compositions" in all of this with types of animals and the occasional stick-like human figure purposefully placed in different locations. Obviously the artists, while enjoying the work for its own sake, must have been motivated by some ritual, symbolic or religious purpose in painting these animals they lived on – for most of the art is devoted to animals. Much ink has been spilled discussing these questions: "At Pèch-Merle," one French critic enthuses, "painting has become an act of incantation, by which man inaugurates the series of great theatrical sanctuaries, in a gesture celebrating the Universe." Be that as it may, the simplest explanation is that this is hunting magic: paint your beast, show him dead or wounded, and you have him. Or the animals could be the totems of the tribes involved. But then there are the strange signs and symbols – hands, dots, wide and narrow shapes – scattered here and there among the paintings. Most agree these may have had sexual significance. It is obvious that this art must have had some symbolic, magical or religious meaning. Beyond that, one guess is probably as good as another.

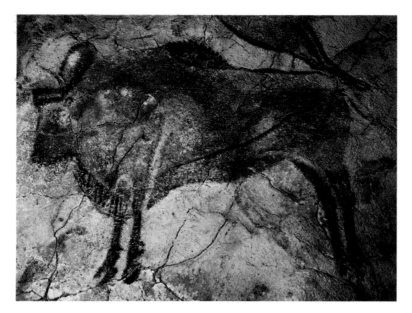

Left A bison painted in red and black from Altamira in northern Spain, another famous cave where numerous bison are painted on the ceiling, all in this very distinctive red and black style. Altamira was one of the first major caves to be discovered, in 1879.

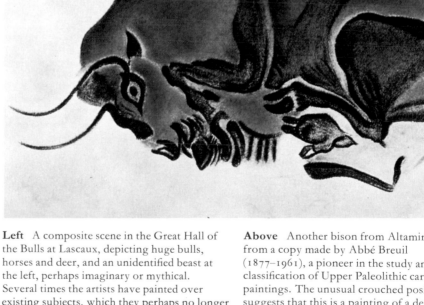

Left A composite scene in the Great Hall of the Bulls at Lascaux, depicting huge bulls, horses and deer, and an unidentified beast at the left, perhaps imaginary or mythical. Several times the artists have painted over existing subjects, which they perhaps no longer considered useful. The bulls are drawn in outline, the horses and deer painted in wash. These are among the finest and largest of all cave paintings, dating from the Solutrean or early Magdalenian period. The largest of the seven bulls is about 18 feet long. Many such scenes were painted deep in the interior of the caves, where no daylight penetrated.

Above Another bison from Altamira, taken from a copy made by Abbé Breuil (1877–1961), a pioneer in the study and classification of Upper Paleolithic carvings and paintings. The unusual crouched position suggests that this is a painting of a dead bison.

Top Bison on the wall of the cave of Niaux, in the French Pyrenees. There is considerable overlap as successive painters have drawn over earlier outlines. Note the two arrows (?) suggestively drawn in the bison body at right.

Above A small horse, also from the cave of Niaux. It dates from the Magdalenian period. With its shaggy coat and short mane, it is magnificently drawn and is of a type similar to the Mongolian wild pony.

Right The "Venus of Laussel" from southwest France, carved in relief on a slab of limestone which probably fell from the shelter wall. She is typical of the numerous female fertility figures, exaggeratedly fat, carved in the round or in relief on stone, bone or ivory, which were widespread in the later Perigordian period. She is carrying a bison horn in her right hand.

Above Outline of a bison's head drawn in soft clay with the fingers on the floor deep inside the Niaux cave, about half a mile from the entrance. Sketches like this reveal the skill of the Magdalenian artist.

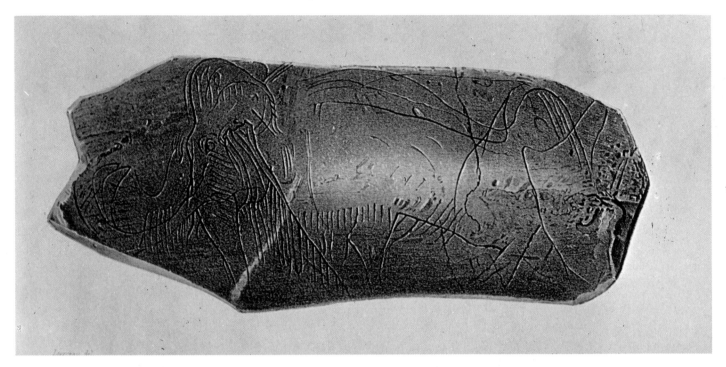

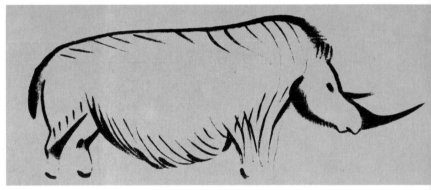

Top A mammoth engraved on a piece of mammoth tusk, found in the cave of La Madeleine in southwest France. This cave gave its name to the style and period called Magdalenian.

Above left Another mammoth, an extinct type of elephant and the principal prey of Upper Paleolithic man in the east. The engraving from a cave wall clearly indicates the long hair and the feet beneath.

Above A woolly rhinoceros, copied from a painting in the cave of Font de Gaume in the Dordogne, southwest France. The original is 27 inches long. Possibly Magdalenian.

Right An exquisite head of a young girl, carved from ivory and probably dating from the Perigordian period. It was found at Brassempouy in France. It is only $1\frac{1}{2}$ inches high.

Above A somewhat crudely drawn mammoth from the cave of Pech-Merle in southwest France, superimposed on a drawing of a cow or bull. Solutrean or early Magdalenian.

Left A Magdalenian horse's head, carved from a bone and dated by excavation to about 12,000 BC.

Below A finely-engraved bison on a piece of limestone. Magdalenian period.

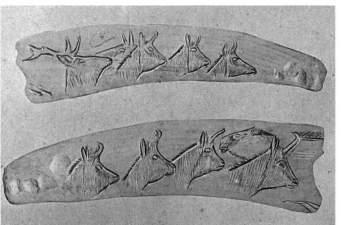

Above left Heads of red deer and ibex engraved on bone tools of the Magdalenian period.

Above Red deer and salmon engraved on a piece of bone. Magdalenian period. Fish supplemented the Stone Age diet.

Left Engraving of a horse. Magdalenian.

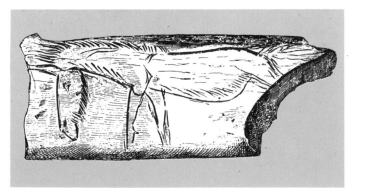

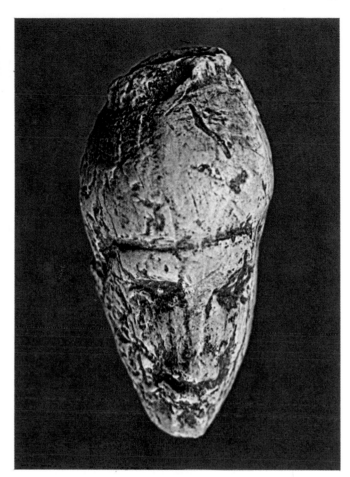

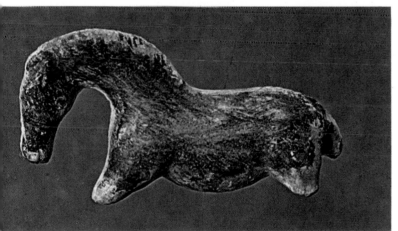

Top left The Venus of Willendorf, a grotesquely fat Gravettian statuette found in Austria. Figurines of this type probably represented mother goddesses – or possibly house goddesses.

Top center This strange carving is thought to represent a highly stylized female figure of the Venus type. **Top right** An ivory head. The face is asymmetrical, and may be a portrait of a person with a facial deformation. Both from Dolni Vistonice, Czechoslovakia.

Above A small ivory horse of the Aurignacian period, found in Germany. Such small animal figures are common in eastern Europe.

Right A crude human figure carved from a mammoth footbone, found in Czechoslovakia; possibly a doll.

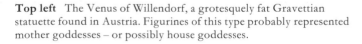

PART SIX

The Past in the Present

SHINTO SHRINES

A living religion of ancient Japan

The Japanese are today perhaps the most eclectic and open-minded people in the world. Their culture, no doubt much affected by their island isolation, is full of contrasts and contradictions. Unlike other peoples they not only tolerate most religions but an individual Japanese may take part in both Shinto practices and Buddhist rituals, while his general conduct may be regulated by Confucian principles or the ethics of Christianity. At the same time he or she may also belong to one of the many "new religions" which have proliferated in Japan in recent years. A marriage might take place in the local Shinto shrine, but when the partners die they may be buried at the family's Buddhist temple. On the one hand, the Japanese hold tenaciously to ancient customs. A man will have his new car blessed at a Shinto shrine, will then drive it to the factory where he works as a skilled electronics engineer, and after work may drive on to a community harvest festival, with dances and merrymaking, which has scarcely altered in 2,000 years. On the other hand, the Japanese, at certain periods in their history have been generously receptive to new ideas from abroad. In the 6th and 7th centuries AD they embraced Buddhism and Chinese culture; and before and after World War II they took to Western ways and technology with far greater success than other Asian peoples. This was not merely imitation; both Buddhism and Western ways were absorbed into the mainstream of Japanese culture. In the 1600s, however, the Japanese deliberately closed their country to outside influences for two and a half centuries, a period which saw, in the West, the beginnings of modern society. When the Japanese joined the world again in the 1850s they found themselves at some disadvantage because of their shaky feudal system and pre-industrial economy. Far from stagnating during their period of isolation, however, they had built up a sense of cultural identity and a degree of self-confidence that enabled them not only to catch up with the Westerners in recent years but even to beat them at their own game.

All this may help to explain the apparent anomaly of the continued existence in modern Japan of a primitive nature religion, Shinto. Some people dispute whether it can be called a religion at all; for Shinto has no dogma, theology or ethical concepts, no visible images, no scripture, and no founder, as do Buddhism and the other religions of Japan. Shinto is derived from the ancient religious practices of very early pre-Buddhist times which involved the worship of a multitude of gods or nature spirits, the *kami*, who could be mythological ancestors or aspects of nature itself such as a tree, a bird, a sacred mountain or a nature god like the sun goddess, presumed ancestor of the emperor. The *kami* are anything that is worshiped or requires ceremonies for its recognition. The name Shinto, "the way of the gods," was given to the religion later to distinguish it from the imported faith of Buddhism. Over the centuries Shinto and Buddhism coexisted in Japan, sometimes in rivalry but more often cooperating with or borrowing from each other. While Buddhism was a highly sophisticated international religion, concerned with salvation and the afterlife, Shinto was and still is strictly Japanese; easy-going, intuitive, it is involved only with the here and now and embodying in its *kami* – there are around 8 million of them! – a feeling of awe and reverence before nature, coupled with the practice of ritual purity. It is not, like Buddhism and Christianity, a personal religion; the *kami* offer protection to the community as a whole. Worship occurs in local, regional and national shrines, as well as annual festivals designed to ensure a good life for all. After the Meiji restoration in the 19th century and up to the end of World War II, Shinto was established as a state cult. It became the medium for an enforced expression of patriotic nationalism, centering around belief in the divinity of the emperor. During World War II this reached frantic heights. But after the defeat of Japan in

Opposite above A typical Shinto shrine. The double-barred entrance gate or *torii* delimits the area sacred to the *kami*, or spirits. Some shrines also have a red arched bridge on the line of approach, as here. Inside the shrine there is a water basin (**below**), presided over here by a dragon representing a water spirit, at which the worshiper purifies himself before his encounter with the *kami* of the shrine.

1945 state Shintoism disappeared. Today there are few worshipers in the Shinto shrines, though many homes still contain simple "god shelves." Shinto survives largely in light-hearted shrine festivals, much like country fairs, the most important of which are the *Kinen* and *Niiname*, spring and autumn festivals concerned with good crops. The autumn feast becomes the union between the male forces of heaven and the female forces of earth. The shrines are still maintained and are visited regularly, though perhaps more by tourists than by believers, and children are still presented at shrines at stated ages. However Shinto is now rather a tradition than a living religion.

Perhaps the most appealing legacy of Shinto is the Japanese love of nature, which is closely linked to Shinto tradition. Most Shinto shrines are found in places of great beauty – near a waterfall, close to a revered mountain, or in a grove of trees. Shrine architecture is deliberately of the simplest, often a series of small wooden buildings set on posts, constructed without nails or complex joints and typified by wide eaves and ridgepole weights – direct descendants of prehistoric granaries. Leading into the

shrine is a *torii*, a gateway with a double crossbeam. The larger shrines are more elaborate, but in any shrine the worshiper first purifies himself, usually by washing out his mouth, then by pulling a bell rope or clapping his hands summons the *kami* to come from their houses in the sky or the earth or near some unusual formation of nature. Communing with the god, he bows in veneration, then sends the god back by another pull at the rope and a clapping of hands. On departing he will leave an offering of the humblest of food, small cups filled with rice, salt and water. Shinto is a humble religion, unstructured, cheerful, devoted to a better life on earth. It is very Japanese.

Shinto is a very earthy religion, concerned with nature and the cycle of the seasons. The *Aoi*, or hollyhock festival (**below**) is held annually in Kyoto on May 15th. At the ancient Omiwa shrine (**opposite**) in Nara prefecture the object of worship is actually Mount Miwa above it. There are several *iwakura*, or rocks, on the mountain which are known as "seats of the *kami*." Certain types of Buddhism in Japan also feature mountain worship cults.

Above Over the centuries Shinto and Buddhism have become thoroughly intermingled. This small Buddhist temple at Ishiyama-dera near Lake Biwa is protected by the symbols of the Shinto *kami*.

Left A pair of rocks "wedded" by a magnificent rope, annually replaced, symbolizes the union of the Sun Goddess and Earth Goddess, who are worshiped nearby in the Grand Shrines of Ise in Mie prefecture, the most sacred of all Japanese shrines and a famous pilgrimage center. Note the Shinto *torii* or gate on the larger rock.

Above The Outer Shrine at Ise, dedicated to the Earth Goddess. This austere structure, rebuilt every 20 years with much ceremony, faithfully reproduces the original shrine, said to have been built here in 478 AD.

Right This small and simple Shinto shrine outside Okayama shows the extended gables and heavy ridgepole weights typical of Shinto architecture. These small wooden buildings derive from Neolithic granaries, set on posts. The type was later used for dwelling houses, then for shrines.

Opposite The Inner Shrine at Ise, the most sacred of the Grand Shrines, is dedicated to the Sun Goddess, reputed ancestor of the Emperor, and contains her sacred mirror. Every Japanese hopes to visit Ise once in a lifetime, and many offerings, such as the *sake* jars shown here, are made at the shrine.

Left top The Sumiyoshi shrine in Osaka is a fine example of Shinto shrine architecture, basically little different from its prototype, the windowless, thatched-roof, raised granary of prehistoric times. This shrine, according to tradition, was founded by the Empress Jingū in the 5th century AD.

Left An example of state Shinto is this impressive shrine, built in Tokyo in 1920 to honor the emperor Meiji, the builder of modern Japan. State Shinto, which disappeared after Japan's defeat in 1945, centered around the concept of the emperor as a divinity.

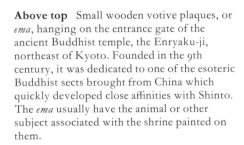

Above top Small wooden votive plaques, or *ema*, hanging on the entrance gate of the ancient Buddhist temple, the Enryaku-ji, northeast of Kyoto. Founded in the 9th century, it was dedicated to one of the esoteric Buddhist sects brought from China which quickly developed close affinities with Shinto. The *ema* usually have the animal or other subject associated with the shrine painted on them.

Above Paper fortune-prayers, bought at a shrine (sometimes from coin machines!), read by the worshiper, then tied to a bush or tree for fulfilment.

Right A snowbound fox, holding the scroll of "ultimate truth" in its mouth, stands in front of the Yoshida shrine in Kyoto. Foxes, representing the messengers of the shrine, mark the many Inari shrines for rice-growing ceremonies which are found all over Japan.

Above Ceremonial dancers perform at the Yasaka shrine in Kyoto. This is part of the great Gion festival held annually in July, which also includes processions of floats in the city streets. The festival dates from 876 AD when it was instituted to help ward off a damaging plague.

DANCE AS RITUAL

A traditional art of Indian Asia

All over Indian Asia the traditional Indian dances still flourish – more vigorously, curiously enough, in Hinduized Southeast Asia than in the mother country. In India Hindu dance is called *Natya*, which means both dance and drama, since everywhere this type of dance is so closely integrated with story-telling, narrative, music and singing that it becomes a single, powerful presentation which aims to delight the eye with color and motion, the ear with sound and the mind with meaning. From southern India come the highly stylized *Kathakali* dance-plays – the passion plays of Hinduism based on the Hindu classics the *Ramayana* or *Mahabharata*. From the north come the religious dramas from Manipura, built out of local folklore and Hindu mythology. In Thailand, Laos, Kampuchea and Burma the dancers, brilliantly costumed in silks and jewels and with golden crowns, may portray the courtship of two lovers or act out long dance dramas, often interspersed with passages of pure, non-narrative dance. In Java the outdoor solo performance of the shadow-puppeteer is widely popular. With the aid of his army of puppets, his gamelan orchestra and female singers and by the light of a flickering lamp, he narrates, chants, sings and speaks the dialogue of his folk story the whole night through. Or there are the majestic court dances of central Java, some masked, some unmasked; while in nearby Bali fearsomely costumed performers, in a deep trance, dance out the ancient battle with the Rangda witch in order to exorcise a village plagued by evil forces. Dance dramas are given in many settings: in village centers, in a theater in Bangkok, in temple courtyards or under the shade of huge tropical trees in Bali. In Kampuchea until recent years dancers of the modern court troupe could be seen in dances that closely echoed those of their Khmer ancestors, the *apsaras*, heavenly dancing girls carved on the walls of Angkor Wat (see above pp. 44–5). Indeed sculpture, the dominant art of Indian Asia in the flourishing medieval period, was closely modeled on the dance and dance drama; one need only examine the stone sculptures of Ellora, the bronzes of southern India, the narrative reliefs on the walls of Angkor in Kampuchea or Borobudur in Java, to confirm this. Both dance and sculpture draw on the same legendary stories from the Indian religious epics; both celebrate the beauty of the human form in motion as an exemplar of the fullness of life on earth, prefiguring the delights of heaven. Shiva himself, the all-encompassing god, the Destroyer, the Preserver, was often lovingly portrayed in his manifestation as *Nataraja*, Lord of the Dance.

The Hindu dance is a living art with very old origins and traditions. The *Bharata Natyam* style of southern India has changed little in the past 300 years and has ancient roots in temple and court dance, but other styles have evolved in very recent years and are still growing. Most traditional dance dramas are peopled with gods, demigods, princes and princesses, but in Indonesia today there are some that dramatize the revolutionary struggle against the Dutch during and after World War II. But all stem from the same roots in Indian thought. Whether the dance is secular or religious, court or temple dance, or is a folk art, almost all of it is in some sense a ritual art, since in Indian aesthetics all the arts – and they are far more closely integrated than in the West – are considered earthly vehicles through which the divine manifests itself in the world. In Indian thought everything in the universe is related to everything else, and a performance of music and dance, the making of a painting or a piece of sculpture – whether earthy and erotic or coolly transcendent like a seated image of a Buddha – is a mythic manifestation of the unity of the whole. The dance was born in the temple as a form of worship and probably originated in the gestures connected with the chanting of the Rig Veda, the oldest of Hindu scriptures. According to legend Brahma himself, the impersonal world spirit, created the dance out of parts of the four original Vedas. By the time of the first great

Indian empire of the Mauryas (3rd century BC) and in later centuries in the opulent, wealthy courts, all the potentates and kings maintained their corps of musicians and dancers. During the golden age of the Guptas (4th–5th centuries AD) dance drama, derived from religious plays, became a secular, courtly art, based on complex rules. The rules are detailed in the first classic manual of the dance drama, the *Natya Shastra* or "Art of the Play." By medieval times every Hindu temple had its dance pavilion in which professional temple dancing girls performed religious dramas for a large public – and probably religious prostitution as well. Much earlier, with the Indian penetration of Southeast Asia between 100 and 1000 AD, Indian dance styles and the Indian historical epics had had a profound impact on each region's dance and drama – though the performing arts of Southeast Asia always kept their own individuality and have grown even further away from Indian styles. In India itself the revival of the traditional Indian dances owes a great deal to the poet Rabindranath Tagore (1861–1941) as well as to the dancer Uday Shankar, who created a modern theater art out of the old classical schools of dance.

Hindu dance follows rigid, traditional rules governing the movement of the eyes, the head, the body, the legs and arms, determining hand gestures, foot positions and even facial expressions. These are so closely adapted to the human anatomy that Westerners sometimes imagine that the art is an easy one. Actually long and rigorous training is required. A competent dancer coordinates the dance so closely with the music that often a large measure of improvisation within the traditional rules is possible. Every movement, every lift of the eyebrow or glance of the eye has a traditional meaning and, with the elaborate costuming and make-up, helps to identify the character being portrayed. As a form of entertainment, as a celebration of life and an emblem of the celestial, the Hindu dance is an embodiment of the best in Indian civilization.

Above An amorous monkey toys with the scarf of a celestial dancer in this voluptuous carving from a 13th-century temple at Belur, in Indian Mysore. The classical Indian artist was obsessed with the dance. His models were actual temple dancers, but his purpose was to bring all people closer to heaven by illustrating the pleasures of celestial life. His art was therefore both transcendent and earthy, even erotic, for to him life and the eternal were one.

Left Heavenly beauties and male dancers cavort joyously to the sounds of music on a frieze from a 13th-century temple in Bombay state, India.

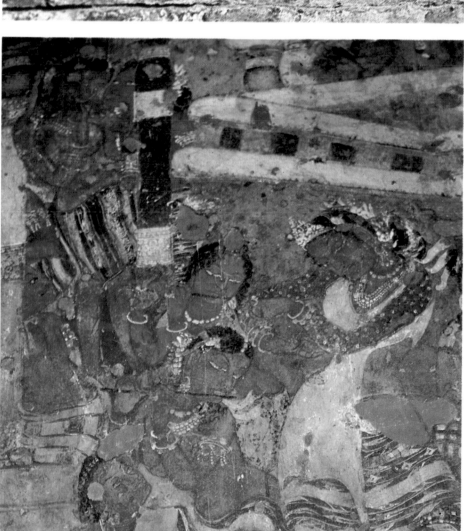

Above A celestial flautist, from an 11th-century temple, Bhuvaneshvara, Orissa, India.

Above left Dancers in postures close to those of modern Indian dancers, on a frieze from the late medieval Indian temple of Chidambaram.

Left A 6th-century fresco from the Buddhist Ajanta caves. The female dancer and musicians were probably modeled on court performers of the day.

Below A modern dancer in the ancient *Bharat Natyam* courtly tradition of southern India illustrates the striking resemblance between Indian dance and sculpture.

Above A 12th-century sculpture from Kampuchea of a celestial girl. The arts of India, with their heady mixture of the earthy and the transcendent, were assimilated in Southeast Asia during the early centuries AD.

Left Dancing *apsaras*, or celestial girls, from the Bayon in Angkor, Kampuchea.

Below left Tranced modern dancers perform the Ketjak in Bali. A chorus of "monkeys" rhythmically chants and sways while reaching out their hands.

Below A modern version of an ancient Thai palace dance, performed on stage in Bangkok.

Above In ancient Angkor Wat a Kampuchean dancer performs a traditional court dance, her fingers curved in a stylized gesture.

Right A vigorous sword dance from the Hindu *Ramayana* story, on a frieze from the Prambanam Shiva temple, Java (c. 900 AD).

Below right A court dancer, portrayed on the huge Buddhist monument of Borobudur in central Java (about 800 AD), entertains her prince and his consort.

Below A dancer in the *Kathakali* tradition of southern India. His elaborate makeup and costume require hours to prepare.

NEAR EASTERN POTTERY

A craft surviving from prehistory

The humble clay pot occupies an important place in the early material culture of mankind all over the world. It was usually the preferred, all-purpose container until metals and eventually plastics took over. It was indispensable in the daily life of its owner, serving for storage and often as a basic item of trade – and it was generally buried with its owner when he or she died. Pottery has always been particularly important in the Near East, the so-called cradle of civilization, because wood, stone and other materials, alternatives to clay in the making of containers, were scarce in much of that area while clay was abundant. Potsherds, too – the pieces left after a pot has been smashed – have by chance also become indispensable in the Near East, at least to the archaeologist intent upon sorting out the intricacies of cultural development from the time mankind first began to settle down and make pottery until historical times. This is because pots were easily broken but their sherds often survived; and when they were painted, as was usually the case in prehistoric periods, their decoration was subject to the laws of fashion and changed very rapidly, as Paris fashions do today. Thus potsherds can be used in archaeology as very precise markers, or tracers, indicating cultural changes or developments as well as connections between one site and another, and relative chronologies. Chipped stone tools form similar markers in exploring the sites of ancient man, but their styles changed much more slowly and covered much larger areas. Of course archaeologists use potsherds in many parts of the world, but in the period of Near Eastern prehistory under consideration here, from about 9000 to 3000 BC, potsherds are exceptionally abundant, indeed they litter the ancient sites, and their decoration was notably brilliant and fast-changing. Moreover the principal cultures of the ancient Near East are usually named after the sites in which the distinctive pottery of each one was first found.

These sites are usually the high mounds or *tells*, so typical of the Near East, which are made up of the remains of mud-brick towns, one lying on top of another like the layers of a cake and providing a roughly chronological stratification as each layer is stripped off to reveal the one beneath it. The remains of each town or culture are usually identified by their distinctive pottery. Even before a mound is excavated, tell-tale sherds scattered on its top will give some indication as to whether or not it is worth digging. For a long time the humble, ubiquitous potsherd has been the basic diagnostic tool of the archaeologist; now, with the perfecting of the new thermoluminescence method of dating sherds, it will become even more important than before.

Why the Near East? It was here that the first agricultural settlements and the first urban civilization appeared. Not that civilization, in different guises, did not arise more or less independently later on in other parts of the world, in Egypt, in China, India, Mexico and Peru. There are indications, too, that the first food crops (millet and rice) may have been raised in Southeast Asia and the first pottery made in Japan, both about 10,000 BC. But it was in the Near East, from Anatolia to the borders of Persia, that the first crucial stirrings of human inventiveness took place, leading to the earliest and probably most influential of all the civilizations With the notable exception of China, the ancient civilization of the Near East has alone maintained an unbroken continuity into modern times, lending its richness to the later cultures of both Europe and Islam. And in the Near East today one may still find local potters, as the following pictures attest, using kilns and making pots much like those being unearthed by the archaeologists, who find comparisons between the modern and ancient products and methods very illuminating. Indeed in this crossroads of many cultures, this ancient land where the desert still impinges on the sown land, where the nomad and the villager still live much as they have always lived, there has been an

Opposite A Turkish potter "throws" a pot on a wheel, using methods very little changed from those developed by his Near Eastern ancestors over 5,000 years ago. He builds up his vessel from a long roll of clay held over his shoulder while rotating the wheel with his foot. Behind him is a pile of freshly-prepared clay.

exciting resurgence, since before World War II, of archaeological exploration – not this time for Sumer and the early civilizations of Mesopotamia, but for the roots of those civilizations, for the traces of the earliest agriculture, pottery and village life in the area. In the ages before the dawn of civilization, of kings, empires and extensive warfare, so much had already been accomplished – agriculture and irrigation, extensive towns with elaborate temples and houses of mud-brick, widespread trade and beautifully fashioned artifacts and pottery.

One of the most decisive steps ever taken by mankind, as he settled into villages, was the domestication of plants and animals; and it was at this time that the first pottery appeared. The earliest known Near Eastern pottery comes from Mureybet in Syria (dated about 8000 BC) and from Iran a little later. The first pottery was handmade, and either sun-dried or lightly fired and thus porous and unsuitable for liquids. With more efficient firing in kilns (developed from bread-making ovens) pottery began to win out over its rivals in other materials and is extensively found after 6000 BC – at first, as at Hassuna, in probably semi-nomadic "camp-sites," and then, with the more developed painted Samarra wares, in the first permanent settlements throughout the country. The slow wheel was in use by the late 5th millennium BC when the Halaf ware, most elegant of all Near Eastern types, was widespread. The Halaf was followed by the Ubaid type which was broadly distributed, indicating the approaching cultural unity which was to produce the great Mesopotamian empires. With Uruk wares (4th millennium BC), mass-produced on a fast wheel and undecorated, we leave the lovely painted wares behind, for we are now at the threshold of that vastly greater cultural and technological widening-out we call civilization.

Below This assemblage of potsherds picked up on the mound of Choga Mami in east central Mesopotamia in 1966, including as it did examples from the pottery styles of all the known prehistoric cultures of the area, led directly to the excavation of the site in 1967–1968. The sherds include fragments of Hassuna, Samarra, Halaf and Ubaid wares. The *tell* was built up between 6000 and 4800 BC.

Above An Afghan potter at work. He is shaping coils of wet clay preparatory to throwing a pot on his wheel. The coiled clay method is well known from ancient times. In the foreground a shaped pot is drying before being fired.

Left The Afghan potter is here shown throwing a pot on his wheel, shaping it with his hands as the wheel is rotated. Potters became a "professional" class of artisans as early as the 6th millennium BC, even before the wheel came into use. The potters of the Near East today are still skilled specialists.

Four stages in the development of Near Eastern prehistoric painted pottery are shown on these pages: Hassuna, the earliest (below), Samarra (opposite above), Halaf (right) and Uruk (opposite below). This lovely Halaf bowl from Arpachiyah (**right**) is typical of the style, which represented the culmination of the art of painted pottery in prehistoric times.

Below A jar from Hassuna, near Nineveh in northern Mesopotamia, an example of the pottery made in the first simple farming communities established in lowland Mesopotamia in the 6th millennium BC. Though still handmade rather than shaped on a wheel, this pot with its carefully incised design is already of high quality.

Above Painted decoration began to come into its own with the exuberant designs of the Samarra period. This sad-eyed female with beauty marks on her cheeks is typical of the style. Samarra ware is characteristic of the first communities who practised intensive irrigation farming in central Mesopotamia in the late 6th millennium BC. It has also been found as far away as Anatolia and southeastern Europe.

Left A group of late Uruk pots from an outpost of the Uruk people far west on the Euphrates in Syria. The style is wholly characteristic of the pots of Uruk itself in Mesopotamia, which in the 4th millennium BC (just before the dawn of civilization) began to be mass-produced on a fast wheel. Decoration is at a minimum. Note the general similarity of these pots to the plain ware still made by the modern potters of Turkey and Afghanistan (previous pages).

Right The last of the painted pottery, this boldly decorated plate belongs to the late Ubaid period, just before painted designs began to disappear in Mesopotamia with the mass-produced Uruk ware. It comes from Woolley's Ur and was found in a deep level below the dynastic city.

Below A bowl with red-on-cream linear designs (about 5000 BC) from Hacilar, a site in the interior of Turkey not far from the Aegean Sea, illustrating how widespread in the Near East during the Neolithic age was the production of painted pottery. The potters of Hacilar were exceptionally skilled, and over a long period.

Left An elaborately-ornamented plate of the 4th millennium BC from Susa in Iran, at the other end of the Near East from Hacilar in Turkey. The skilled Iranian potters continued to produce imaginatively-decorated painted wares far longer than their counterparts in the lowlands of Mesopotamia.

Left below An attractive beaker from western Iran, in the Sialk style, also 4th millennium BC. Animals, often ibexes (as here) or goats, were often depicted by these potters, and the "skidding" position was typical of their art.

Above Did the ancient potters have a sense of humor? On this Samarra period pot from Choga Mami, defecating ibexes are surrounded by centipedes and swastikas. These potters were the first to make extensive use of animal designs.

Right The intricate beauty of Halaf painted pottery designs is illustrated in this rendering of a polychrome plate, one of a group found at Arpachiyah in what is thought to have been a potter's workshop. Arpachiyah seems to have been an artisans' village serving the much larger settlement nearby on the Tigris River which eventually became Nineveh. The workshop had been burned and the pottery deliberately smashed.

Below The Samarra period potters were the first to decorate their wares with human figures. These male and female "dancing figures," a common motif, adorn a very late Samarra style bowl of about 5000 BC.

Left Animal designs appeared earlier than the human figures. This vigorously-drawn cobra with double fangs appears on a very early Halaf fragment from Arpachiyah. It dates from the late 6th millennium BC.

Below Two more early Halaf potsherds, decorated with a very common motif of bulls' heads. A bull's head or bukrania motif often occurs throughout the Near East, notably in the great Neolithic town of Çatal Hüyük in Turkey, and bulls were portrayed in many ways in the much later Minoan civilization of Crete. Undoubtedly they were, as always, a symbol of virility.

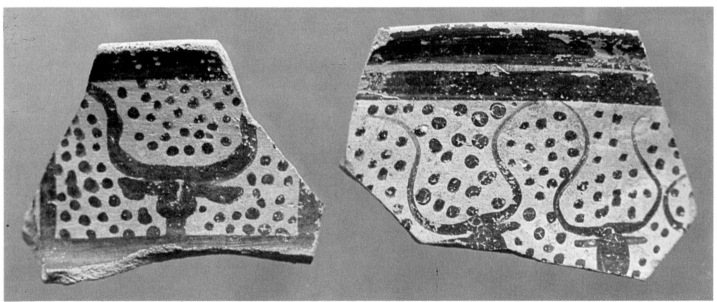

BUTSER HILL

An Iron Age farm re-created

Experimental archaeologists are a small but devoted band of enthusiasts who believe that it is not enough just to dig up the material remains of the remote past and then puzzle over their meaning, the usual task of the archaeologist. Experimental archaeologists believe in making actual use of the tools and weapons of the ancients, reconstructing their houses, cultivating the crops known to them, duplicating their pottery by making it in reconstructed kilns, all in carefully controlled experiments. They hope to learn "how it was done" by doing it, and to generate new ideas in the process. They seldom expect definite answers, but they hope to learn a lot – and some of it quite unexpected. In the process of constructing the central roundhouse at Butser Hill Iron Age farm, for instance, the builders discovered that a central post, usually thought by the archaeologists to be essential in holding the structure together, was in fact not required for stability. A small point, but a useful one in a field which at best must depend upon "the disciplined use of the imagination." As Dr John Coles of Cambridge University, the leading authority in the field, writes, experimental archaeology is able to contribute to its mother discipline "a range of possible solutions to archaeological problems of interpretation." These are, necessarily, mostly in the areas of technology and subsistence. Experimental archaeology is a strenuous and exciting discipline, and therefore the activity is often filmed for television. If, for instance, you are testing the potentialities of a flint arrowhead it is better, though more dangerous, to shoot at a real bear in the field than at a pillow or target on your lawn. And if it will further the cause for a group of volunteers to live for a year, as happened in England in 1977, in the ungrateful environment of a simulated Iron Age village, cut off from the world, building their own huts with Iron Age tools and providing for their own food, then let it be done.

Experimental archaeology is as old as archaeology itself. As soon as the first huge Late Bronze Age horns of northern Europe were discovered in 1797, there were attempts to play them. A 19th-century Dublin doctor who tried to sound an Irish horn of the same period, burst a blood vessel and died a few days later, a martyr to the cause. Experimental archaeology has its modern hero in Thor Heyerdahl, who sailed the balsa-wood raft *Kon-Tiki* across the Pacific and the reed-built *Ra-II* across the Atlantic.

One of the most ambitious of experimental archaeology's projects has been the Butser Hill Experimental Farm, in Hampshire, England, the brainchild of Peter Reynolds, its director. It is not a one-year experiment but an attempt to recreate a working Iron Age farm and to monitor its progress over a 10- to 20-year period, entailing the reconstruction of several different types of farm buildings, based upon excavated examples, the cultivation of cereal crops actually grown in the Iron Age, the study of yield figures and the field boundaries (lynchets) that result from annual cultivation, the raising of domesticated livestock including cattle, sheep, horses and fowl of early breeds, and a variety of related activities like weaving, potting, charcoal burning and smelting. Already radical new interpretations of known Iron Age problems have emerged from the project. Moreover Butser Hill is both an experimental laboratory and an open-air museum for those who are interested.

The progress of experimental archaeology has been marked not only by the setting up of such long-term projects as Butser Hill Farm but also by many experiments of a more bizarre or colorful nature. In the 1930s an English bandsman, brought to Cairo to try to play Tutankhamun's trumpet, produced a lovely fanfare, heard by thousands over the radio. Only later was it revealed that he had inserted his own mouthpiece into the ancient instrument. In 1950, when the almost perfectly-preserved body of Tollund Man (1st century BC) was

Opposite The farmstead, a roundhouse, centers the Butser Hill Experimental Farm in Hampshire, England which simulates a Celtic farm of about 300 BC. The roundhouse was built on the exact plan of an Iron Age house excavated in Dorset, known only from its postholes cut into the clay. At Butser Iron Age crops are grown experimentally, including woad (**below**) from which was derived the famous blue dye of Iron Age warriors.

discovered in a Danish peat bog, the experimenters analyzed the contents of his stomach to find that his last meal had been a vegetarian feast. Gathering together the same seeds and plants, they brewed them up into an "oily-looking concoction" which tasted better than it looked. More recently several young Smithsonian scientists were to be observed on a hillside near Washington, D.C., casting stone-tipped spears into the carcass of a dead zoo elephant, then cutting up the bloody mess with stone knives, the whole operation being elaborately recorded on tape and with a potentiometer to record the effort. The object? To find out how prehistoric Americans of 10,000 years ago killed and butchered their mammoths. The stone tools and points, incidentally, were made by a student of Don Crabtree of Idaho State University, a widely-known craftsman skilled in "replicating" ancient stone artifacts. In another experiment, two shields of the type used by contending warriors of Late Bronze Age England were reconstructed – one of leather and one of bronze. These were then assaulted with Bronze Age spears and swords. Unexpectedly, the leather stood up to the attack far better than the thin sheet bronze.

There have also been many less spectacular experiments, for example in the clearing of forests with stone, bronze and iron tools, showing not only that in his small way prehistoric man was already adept in destroying his environment, but that in certain circumstances stone axes were as efficient as modern ones, and certainly better than those of bronze. Experiments to find out how early earthworks stood up to soil erosion, to discover how large stone monuments like Stonehenge or Maya Uxmal were built, how copper was smelted and how Romano-British pots were fired, the time it takes to skin a small deer with a flint knife (about 15 minutes), or how the Egyptians made papyrus paper, have all been useful. But now to return to Butser Hill and the Iron Age.

The roundhouse has two circles of posts (**above**), the inner and taller circle bearing the weight of the roof. These posts were joined by lintels, to which the main rafters were fastened (**opposite**), then the base for the thatching was lashed onto the notched rafters (**right**). Meanwhile the walls had been wattled with hazel rods and daubed with a clay mixture while the thatching (**far right**) was completed. This rather sophisticated farmhouse, seen (**below**) dressed for a television show, was surrounded by a ditch (**below right**) with a strong wattle fence above its inner side. The whole job was accomplished by a crew of young archaeologists under the direction of Peter Reynolds. Learning "how it was done by doing it," they also solved many problems of general interest to excavators.

Left A simple upright loom employed for weaving cloth for garments and other uses. The type has been guessed at from the bobbins and loom weights found in Iron Age excavations, as well as occasional loom posthole emplacements.

Left Making pottery was probably the responsibility of the women of the village. Volunteers are here shown fashioning pots by hand preparatory to firing them in a kiln. The fast wheel was not known in Britain until the 1st century BC. Grain grown at Butser is ground in a rotary quern (**below**), being fed into the hole in the upper stone. The flour issues from between the rotating stones, and is then stored in pit silos, of which there are a number at Butser, or is baked in a clay oven like that in the interior of the farmstead (**below left**). Near the oven is a screen for the hearth and a loom emplacement. Drying woad hangs from the rafters.

Left Peter Reynolds guides his Dexter cattle, which approximate Iron Age breeds, as they pull a primitive plow. Note the second, smaller roundhouse next to the main farmstead. Small Soay sheep from Saint Kilda Island off northwest Scotland, again close to Iron Age types, are also kept at Butser as well as undeveloped types of pigs and chickens. The Soay sheep, bred for their wool, are difficult to control and are not unlike small goats. Primitive wheats include both spelt and emmer (**top left**) which are grown under differing conditions to test their yield figures.

FURTHER READING

Western Europe

Breuil, Henri, *Four Hundred Centuries of Cave Art* Montignac, 1952.
Ucko, P. J., and Rosenfeld, A., *Palaeolithic Cave Art* London, 1967.
Waechter, J., *Man Before History* Oxford, 1976.
Harding, D. W., *Prehistoric Europe* Oxford, 1976.
Piggot, S., *Ancient Europe* Edinburgh, 1973.
Daniel, G. E., *The Megalith Builders of Western Europe* London, 1958.
Renfrew, C. (ed.), *British Prehistory: A New Outline* London, 1974.

Greece and Italy

Warren, P., *The Aegean Civilizations* Oxford, 1976.
Hood, M. S. F., *The Home of the Heroes. The Aegean before the Greeks* London, 1967.
Higgins, R., *Minoan and Mycenaean Art* London and New York, 1967.
Johnston, A., *The Emergence of Greece* Oxford, 1976.
Ling, R., *The Greek World* Oxford, 1976.
Bury, J. B., and Meiggs, R., *A History of Greece to the Death of Alexander the Great* 4th edn., London, 1975.
Flacelière, R., *Daily Life in Greece at the Time of Pericles* London, 1965.
Richter, G. M. A., *A Handbook of Greek Art* 7th edn., London, 1974.
Cook, R. M., *Greek Painted Pottery* 2nd edn., London, 1972.
Lawrence, A. W., *Greek Architecture* 3rd edn., Harmondsworth, 1973.
Rostovtzeff, M. I., *Social and Economic History of the Hellenistic World* 3 vols., Oxford, 1941.
Pallottino, M., *The Etruscans* London, 1975.
Vickers, M., *The Roman World* Oxford, 1977.
Starr, C. G., *The Ancient Romans* New York, 1971.
Balsdon, J. P. V. D., *Rome, the Story of an Empire* London, 1977.
Balsdon, J. P. V. D., *Life and Leisure in Ancient Rome* New York, 1969.
Strong, D. E., *Roman Art* London, 1976.

The Near East

David, R., *The Egyptian Kingdoms* Oxford, 1975.
Gardiner, A. H., *Egypt of the Pharaohs* Oxford, 1961.
Edwards, I. E. S., *The Pyramids of Egypt* London, 1961.
Desroches-Noblecourt, C., *Tutankhamen* London, 1971.
Stevenson Smith, W., *The Art and Architecture of Ancient Egypt* London, 1958.
Oates, D. and J., *The Rise of Civilization* Oxford, 1976.
Postgate, N., *The First Empires* Oxford, 1977.
Kramer, S. H., *The Sumerians* Chicago, 1963.
Lloyd, S., *The Art of the Ancient Near East* London, 1961.
Moorey, P. R. S., *Biblical Lands* Oxford, 1975.
Collins, R., *The Medes and the Persians* London, 1974.

Wilber, D. N., *Persepolis* London, 1969.
Hermann, G., *The Iranian Revival* Oxford, 1977.
Ghirshman, R., *Iran, Parthians and Sasanians* London, 1962.
Rogers, M., *The Spread of Islam* Oxford, 1976.
Creswell, K. A. C., *The Muslim Architecture of Egypt* 2 vols., Oxford, 1952, 1959.

India and the Far East

Rawson, P. S., *Indian Asia* Oxford, 1977.
Basham, A. L. (ed.), *A Cultural History of India* Oxford, 1975.
Swaan, W., *Lost Cities of Asia* London, 1966.
Zimmer, H., *The Art of Indian Asia* New York, 1955.
Rawson, P. S., *The Art of Southeast Asia* London and New York, 1967.
FitzGerald, C. P., *Ancient China* Oxford, 1978.
Li, Dun J., *The Civilization of China* New York, 1975.
FitzGerald, C. P., *China: A Short Cultural History* rev. edn., London, 1976.
Sullivan, M., *A Short History of Chinese Art* London, 1967.
The Genius of China, catalogue of an exhibition of archaeological finds from the People's Republic of China, London, 1974.
Kidder, J. E., *Ancient Japan* Oxford, 1977.
Hall, J. W., *Japan, from Prehistory to Modern Times* Tuttle, Tokyo and Rutland, Vt., 1971.
Kidder, J. E., *Early Buddhist Japan* London and New York, 1972.
Ponsonby-Fane, R. A. B., *Studies in Shinto and Shrines* Kyoto, 1956.

Africa

Garlake, P. S., *The Kingdoms of Africa* Oxford, 1978.
Davidson, B., *Africa: History of a Continent* London, 1966.
Fagg, W., *Nigerian Images* London, 1963.
Willett, F., *Ife in the History of West African Sculpture* London, 1967.
Dark, P. J. C., *An Introduction to Benin Art and Technology* Oxford, 1973.
Garlake, P. S., *Great Zimbabwe* London, 1973.

The New World

Swanson, E. H., Bray, W., and Farrington, I., *The New World* Oxford, 1975.
Sanders, W. T., and Price, B. J., *Mesoamerica: The Evolution of a Civilization* New York, 1968.
Weaver, M. P., *The Aztecs, Maya and their Predecessors* New York, 1972.
Bushnell, G. H. S., *Peru* London, 1956.
Kendall, A., *Everyday Life of the Incas* London and New York, 1973.
Hemming, J., *The Conquest of the Incas* London, 1970.

ACKNOWLEDGMENTS

Aerofilms, Boreham Wood 86 top right, 86 bottom right.

Anglo-Chinese Educational Institute, London 208/209, 210 top left.

Ashmolean Museum, Oxford 82 bottom, 128 top right, 128 bottom right, 129 top, 129 bottom left, 130 top left, 130 top right, 130 centre, 130 bottom left, 130 bottom right, 131 left, 131 centre, 131 right, 132 left, 273 top left, 273 bottom left.

Badisches Landesmuseum, Karlsruhe 21 bottom right.

Dick Barnard, London 36 bottom right, 48 bottom, 68, 74 centre, 79 top, 107 centre right, 162 botom left.

Bibliothèque Nationale, Paris 158 top.

Bijutsu Shuppan-sha, Tokyo 220 top right, 221.

E. Böhm, Mainz 110 bottom, 112/113 bottom left, 112 bottom right, 115 top.

W. Bray, London 53 top.

British Museum, London 58, 59 top, 62 bottom, 63 bottom, 74 bottom, 162 top left, 164, 270 top right.

A. M. Calverley, *The Temple of King Sethos I at Abydos*, 1938, Chicago 98 left, 98 top right, 98 bottom right.

P. Cheze-Brown, London 30 centre right, 30 bottom.

Colorific! London 30 centre left.

Corpus Christi College, Cambridge 165 top.

Douglas Dickins, London 41, 42 top left, 42 top right, 43 bottom, 44 bottom, 45, 263 top right, 263 bottom right, 264 top left, 264 bottom left, 264 bottom right, 265 top left, 265 top right, 265 bottom left.

C. M. Dixon, Dover 87 top right, 87 bottom left, 87 bottom right, 192 bottom right, 193 top, 193 bottom centre, 193 bottom right.

Eastfoto, New York 148 top.

École Française d'Archéologie, Athens 106 bottom left.

Egypt Exploration Society, London 99.

Ekdotike Athenon S.A., Athens 36 bottom left (National Archaeological Museum, Athens), 37 top (Delos Archaeological Museum), 70/71, 72 bottom left, 121 bottom, 123 top right, 123 centre right, 124 top left, 124 top right, 125 bottom, 158 bottom (National Archaeological Museum, Athens), 161 top left (National Archaeological Museum, Athens), 163 (National Archaeological Museum, Athens), 167 bottom left (National Archaeological Museum, Athens), 230, 232 bottom, 234/235 top, 234/235 bottom, 235, 236, 237.

A. A. M. van der Heyden, Amsterdam 19, 20 bottom, 24 top, 24 bottom left, 25 left, 73 bottom, 75, 78 bottom left, 78 bottom right, 80 bottom right, 81 top left, 81 top right, 91 top left, 92 top, 92 bottom left, 92 bottom right, 93 top right, 93 bottom centre, 94 top, 94 bottom left, 95 top, 95 bottom left, 95 bottom right, 96 top left, 96 bottom right, 96 bottom left, 97 top right, 97 bottom left, 97 bottom right, 102 bottom, 104 right, 107 top right, 123 top left, 123 centre left, 161 centre left, 194, 197 top, 198 bottom, 199 top, 199 bottom, 250 bottom.

Michael Holford, London 2–3 (British Museum), 63 top right (British Museum), 66 top, 72/73, 73 top, 74 top left, 160 centre left, 160 bottom left, 160 bottom right, 161 bottom right (British Museum), 167 top left (British Museum), 200/201, 212 top (British Museum), 214 bottom right (Musée Guimet, Paris), 241 top left.

Holle Bildarchiv, Baden-Baden 49, 88, 118, 134 bottom, 198 top left.

Angelo Hornak, London 80 top right, 80 bottom left.

Iraq Museum, Baghdad 271 top.

A. Kendal 47 top, 51 bottom right, 53 bottom, 54 top, 54 bottom.

F. L. Kennett, London 133, 135 top right.

V. Kennett, London 50 top, 51 top, 51 bottom left, 52 top, 52 bottom, 215 top right, 263 top left.

J. Edward Kidder Jr., Tokyo 253, 255 top, 256 bottom right, 258 top left, 258/259 top right, 259 bottom left.

L'Abbé Breuil/Arnold Fawcus, Paris 241 centre right, 244 centre right.

Lartet and Christy, *Reliquiae Aquitancicae* 244 top.

J. Lavaud, Paris 125 top left.

Andrew Lawson, Charlbury 272 top (British Museum), 272 top left (British Museum), 275 bottom (British Museum).

Andrew Lawson/J. Waechter 245, 246 top left, 246 centre left, 247 top right, 247 bottom left, 247 bottom right.

B. Leimbach, Reading 46 top.

Lucy Lim, New York 172 top right.

Lesley A. Ling, Manchester 167 bottom right.

Lovell Johns, Oxford 29 top left.

Howard Loxton, London 18 bottom, 34/35, 36 top left, 106 top left, 233 top left.

Mansell Collection, London 161 top right, 166 top, 166 bottom (Louvre).

Leonard von Matt, Buochs 14, 18 top, 22 top, 22 bottom, 23, 24 bottom left (Pompeii Museum), 25 right, 180 top, 184/5 centre.

Yvonne McClean, London 31 bottom left, 31 bottom right.

William McQuitty, London 150 bottom right, 153 top, 168 bottom, 171 left, 171 right (Peking Museum), 174 top right (British Museum), 174 bottom (Musée Cernuschi, Paris), 177 top, 179 left (Musée Cernuschi, Paris), 179 right (Musée Cernuschi, Paris).

Elsevier Archives, Amsterdam 42 bottom left (Ewing Galloway), 91 bottom right, 106 top right, 107 left, 117 bottom left, 132 top right, 132 bottom right, 134 top, 135 top left, 135 centre left, 135 bottom left, 161 centre right, 196 bottom, 197 bottom right, 233 bottom left.

W. B. Emery (after *Archaic Egypt*) 196 centre.

284 · ACKNOWLEDGMENTS

George Eogan, Dublin 188 top, 188 bottom, 191 top left, 191 top right, 191 bottom left, 191 bottom right.

Robert Estall, London 82 top, 87 top left.

Fairman (after *Worship and Festival*) 90 top, 90 bottom.

F. Fanelli, *Atene Attica*, 1707; photo R. Wilkins 66 bottom.

I. Farrington, Canberra 50 bottom.

Federal Bureau of Antiquities, Nigeria 222 bottom.

E. Flandin, *Voyage en Perse*, 1843–47; by courtesy of The Bodleian Library, Oxford 138–9 bottom.

Alain Fournier, Blois 242 top right, 242 bottom left, 243, 244 bottom left.

John Freeman, London 76 top, 81 bottom (both by kind permission of John Harvey).

Ray Gardner, London 136 bottom (British Museum).

Peter Garlake, London 26, 28, 29 bottom left, 30 top right, 225 top left, 225 top right, 227 top right, 227 bottom left.

J. Paul Getty Museum, Malibu 21 top.

Giraudon, Paris 162 centre right (Louvre).

Roger Gorringe,London 85 top right, 103 top left, 122 top, 149 top right, 192 top right, 233 right, 274 top right.

Basil Gray, Abingdon 207 top left.

Richard and Sally Greenhill, London 206 bottom, 211, 220 bottom left (British Museum).

F. Guaman Poma de Ayala, *Nueva Coronica y Buen Gobierno* 46 bottom.

Dennis Harding, Edinburgh 276 top, 278 bottom, 279 top left, 279 centre left, 279 centre right, 279 bottom left, 279 bottom right, 281 bottom centre.

Robert Harding Associates, London 34 top, 44 top left, 62 top (British Museum), 69 bottom, 74 top right, 105, 140 top, 143 centre, 146 top, 146 bottom, 150 top, 150 bottom left, 151 top, 152, 153 bottom right, 154 bottom right, 155, 170 bottom, 172 bottom, 173 top, 173 bottom centre, 173 bottom right, 176 top centre, 176 bottom centre, 176/177 bottom right, 177 bottom, 220 top left (British Museum), 252, 254/255, 256 top, 257, 258 bottom left, 258/259 centre right, 269 top, 269 bottom.

D. Harrisiadis, Athens 104 top left, 121 top left.

Hauptstaatsarchiv, Stuttgart 31 top left, 31 top right.

Georgina Herrmann, Oxford 136 top, 138 centre right, 139 top, 140 centre left, 140 bottom right, 141 bottom, 142 top, 142 bottom, 143 centre left, 143 top right, 143 bottom right, 144 top, 144 bottom, 145.

Moravské Muzeum, Brno 247 top centre.

Caecilia H. Moessner (Staatliche Museum, Munich) 62 bottom right.

Musée des Antiquités, St. Germaine-en-Laye 242 bottom left.

Musée du Périgord, Périgueux (© Arch/Phot. S.P.A.D.E.M., Paris 1980) 240 bottom.

Museum für Völkerkunde (Staatliche Museen Preussischer Kulturbesitz), Berlin 222 top.

National Palace Museum, Taipei 204, 207 centre, 208 left, 209 left, 210.

National Tourist Organization of Greece, London 120 top right.

Naturhistorisches Museum, Vienna 247 top left.

Howard Nelson, London 153 bottom left, 154 top, 168 top.

D. & J. Oates, London 268 bottom, 271 bottom, 273 bottom right, 274 bottom.

Oriental Institute, University of Chicago 112/113 top, 115 bottom, 116 top, 116 centre, 116 bottom right, 117 top.

Oxford Illustrators 29 top right, 87 centre, 114 top, 149 bottom right, 190 bottom right.

John Picton, London 226 bottom left, 229 bottom right.

Picturepoint, London 29 bottom right, 35 top right, 259 top left, 270 bottom (Iraq Museum, Bagdad).

E. Piette, *L'Art pendant L'Age du Renne* 246 centre right.

Josephine Powell, Rome 272 bottom (Ankara Museum).

Mauro Pucciarelli, Rome 16/17, 180 bottom (Time Inc., from Time-Life, Emergence of Man), 182 bottom (Time Inc., from Time-Life, Emergence of Man), 183 top, 183 bottom (Time Inc., from Time-Life, Emergence of Man), 184 top left, 185 top right (Time Inc., from Time-Life, Emergence of Man), 185 bottom right, 186 (Vatican Museums), 187 top (Vatican Museums), 187 bottom (Time Inc., from Time-Life, Emergence of Man), 215 bottom centre (Victoria & Albert Museum), 262 top right (British Museum), 263 bottom left (British Museum).

P. Rawson, Durham 212 bottom.

Peter J. Reynolds, East Meon, Hants. 276 bottom, 280 top, 280 bottom, 281 top left, 281 centre, 281 bottom right.

Rijksmuseum, Amsterdam 260.

Michael Roaf, Cambridge 144 bottom.

J. M. Rogers, London 76 bottom.

Royal Ontario Museum, Toronto 174 top left, 178.

Scala, Florence 59 bottom (Baghdad), 60/61 (Baghdad), 60 (Baghdad), 61 (Baghdad), 63 top left (Baghdad), 214 bottom left, 215 top left, 215 bottom right, 216 top, 216 bottom left (Prince of Wales Museum, Bombay), 216 bottom right (Birmingham Museum), 218 top right (Ayutthaya Museum), 219 bottom left (National Museum, Bangkok), 219 bottom right (National Museum, Bangkok), 264 top right (Musée Guimet, Paris).

R. Schoder, Chicago 37 bottom, 72 top (British Museum), 72 bottom right (National Archaeological Museum, Athens), 103 bottom, 165 bottom left (Musée de Châtillon-sur-Seine).

Schwitter Photo Library, Leili 266

Servizio Editoriale Fotografico, Turin 238.

R. Sheridan, Harrow 80 top left.

G. Speake, Oxford 34 bottom, 36 top right.

Spectrum, London 32, 35 top left, 55, 100 top, 104 centre left, 123 bottom left, 250 top.

Francis Speed, Calabar 226 top left, 226 top right, 226 bottom right, 227 top left, 227 centre right.

Staatliche Graphische Sammlung, Munich 21 bottom left.

Wolf Suschitsky, London 43 top right, 44 top centre.

Joanna Tanlaw 175 (Shensi Provincial Museum), 176/177 top right, 176 bottom left (Shensi Provincial Museum).

C. Thurston-Shaw, Cambridge 224 bottom.

University of Cambridge, C'tee for Aerial Photography 190 bottom left, 192 bottom left.

Louis Vanden Berghe, Ghent 141 top.

M. Vickers, Oxford 20 top.

Visual Art Productions, London 40.

J. Waechter 246 top right, 246 bottom left.

P. Warren, Bristol 125 centre right.

Werner Forman, London 69 top, 207 bottom left, 217 bottom left, 265 bottom right.

Frank Willett, Glasgow 225 bottom left, 225 bottom right.

Roger Wood, London 110 top.

Zefa, London 30 top left, 38, 43 top left, 44 top right, 151 bottom right, 215 bottom left (Sarnath Museum), 217 top left, 217 centre right, 218 top left, 218 bottom left, 219 top right, 262 bottom left.

INDEX